creative ESSENTIALS

Other Kamera Books titles by David Carter

Plays... and how to produce them
The Western
East Asian Cinema
Georges Simenon
Literary Theory

David Carter

THE ART OF ACTING

... And How to Master It

creative ESSENTIALS

First published in 2010 by Kamera Books

PO Box 394, Harpenden, Herts, AL5 1XJ

www.kamerabooks.com

Copyright © David Carter 2010

Series Editor: Hannah Patterson

A CIP catalogue record for this book is available from the British Library.

ISBN 978-1-84243-221-1

2 4 6 8 10 9 7 5 3 1

Typeset by Avocet Typeset, Chilton, Aylesbury, Bucks

Printed by J.F. Print, Sparkford, Somerset

ACKNOWLEDGEMENTS

The principal debt of gratitude owed by the author is to the numerous actors and actresses, those living and those who have long since made their final exits, and whose utterances have been scoured and analysed. I have diligently read between their lines for clues to the mystery of their art. Another major debt, as always, is owed to my ever-scrupulous editors.

CONTENTS

INTRODUCTION

You cannot learn how to become an actor by reading a book. Many actors would also argue that you cannot, in any case, teach someone how to act. Yet countless books on the topic exist and hundreds of institutions offer training courses for would-be actors. This should be no surprise, for the situation is the same in the practice of all the arts, to a greater or lesser degree. One cannot become an actor without certain psychological preconditions, though these do not predetermine one to become an actor. The basic propensity has to be nurtured, and it is in this secondary process that reading and training can play a role.

It is also often said that the difference between amateur and professional actors is one of technique, though what this technique consists of is usually left vague. It will be perceived in the course of the present book that the techniques in question are, amongst other things, the nurture and use of the voice, the control of breathing, and the precise physical control of the body. Also, every professional actor has to learn how to maintain stamina through long performances and through long runs. All of these accomplishments are not, of course, out of the reach of the amateur, if they have the time to devote to acquiring them.

For amateur and would-be professional alike, the present book aims to provide a basic introduction to the kinds of attitudes, mental processes and other abilities which are necessary if one wishes to develop and mature as an actor.

The author is modest concerning his own experience and abilities: countless years as both actor and director in an amateur drama group and a lifelong enthusiasm for all-things-theatrical have lent him the courage to express his convictions. Many people, especially directors, have spoken disparagingly of the average thespian's inability to be articulate about what they do, but the author is convinced that, if anyone can reveal the secrets of the actor's art, it is surely those who practise it successfully and well. This book is therefore based on the opinions and feelings of many well-known actors and actresses about all the major aspects of their work. The conclusions and advice provided are therefore very much based on their reflections.

The two main sections of this book are noticeably different in character, but there is a logical connection and development between them. The first section traces the history of acting styles and techniques through the ages, with an emphasis on descriptions of what performances in past ages were like and what principles governed them. It will be demonstrated that all acting styles fall somewhere on a continuum between naturalism and artificiality, with preferences for one tendency over the other varying from age to age and culture to culture. The usefulness of this section to the modern actor is in providing some awareness of the traditions behind present vogues in acting styles. Many recognised great actors, such as Laurence Olivier, have acknowledged how they developed their own styles of acting from familiarity with the acting styles of the past. Each new generation of actors takes what it admires from great acting of yesteryear and reacts against those elements which now seem hackneyed or inappropriate. Acting, as with many processes in history, is a dialectic between extremes, with the styles of older generations always both inspiring new generations and provoking them to change. A history of this dialectic process also serves to remind every aspiring actor that in the theatre, too, there is nothing new under the sun.

Furthermore, an awareness of what styles of acting prevailed in particular periods and for certain kinds of plays is crucial when preparing to act a role in a period piece: a play written in highly stylised language will not lend itself easily to naturalistic playing.

The focus then shifts in the second section to the tasks facing every actor and the skills it is necessary to master. The general goals and ideals, realism and truth, are considered first, and the methods of preparing a role, including considerations of methods developed by the most influential theorist of acting technique, Konstantin Stanislavsky. Some consideration is then given to the technical control of the voice and the need to respect the structure of the language. Important issues relating to the process of rehearsing a play are explored, as is the actor's relationship to the audience. Certain special concerns are then considered, such as acting for films and television, differences between national styles, and handling the language of Shakespeare's plays.

In the third section, advice is provided for those readers who are seriously considering becoming professional actors, and the importance of good training is stressed.

The Resources section contains information on books dealing with the main aspects of acting covered in the present book, together with advice on publications which are especially useful for would-be professionals.

Those wishing to seek further advice about setting up a drama group and organising productions are recommended to read a companion volume in the Creative Essentials series by the same author and entitled *Plays... And How to Produce Them*.

Finally, if this book has served to help a few people discover the actor in their soul, it will have served its purpose well.

THE HISTORY OF ACTING STYLES AND TECHNIQUES

Surveying what has been written over the ages by actors, dramatists, critics and philosophers, it is clear, from the descriptions, that all acting styles fall somewhere along a continuum between what may loosely be called the Natural and the Artificial. Various other aspects of acting have been given close consideration over the years, according to the concerns of the day, such as gesture, movement, elocution, etc, but most assessments of actors' performances usually attempt to rate them as being somewhere between convincingly realistic or natural and highly stylised and artificial. The terms 'realistic' and 'natural' do not always denote praise; nor do the terms 'stylised' and 'artificial' always denote criticism. It tends to depend on the writer's own preferences and the tastes of the era.

In the following survey the concern has constantly been to focus on the styles of acting encouraged and the techniques employed to attain them. Accounts of actual dramatists and their works, and the modes of theatrical production, are therefore only included where of relevance to understanding the acting styles. For similar reasons, the traditions in some countries are only dealt with cursorily or not at all, relevance to the development of acting theory and styles being always the only criterion. Also, as the purpose of this book is to provide advice to would-be actors in the English-speaking world, and in what may be loosely described as the western theatrical tradition, all consideration of acting traditions in the Far and Near East, and in Africa, India and South America have been excluded, with the occasional exception of allusions by specific exponents of the theory and practice of acting.

THE CLASSICAL PERIOD

Greece

Although dramatic performances of some kind doubtless occurred in earlier ages, and most likely among the Egyptians, most accounts of the history of drama and of acting start with reference to the tragic drama of the Greeks developed from the recitation of dithyrambs and ritual choral dances in celebration of the god Dionysus, the god of wine and fertility. The very first actor whose name has come down to posterity is Thespis, who is reported to have stepped aside from the choral narration with its leader and impersonated one of the characters in the story being told. Whatever the facts of the matter, his name has been transmuted into an epithet for all those who indulge in dramatic performance: Thespians.

Interesting to note is that, from the very beginning, the art practised by Thespis had its negative critics. Thespis was also a dramatist, and when he brought one of his productions, in which he also acted, to Athens, he was condemned by the lawgiver Solon for his dangerous and deceptive impersonations. The birth of the first known acting performance therefore coincided with that of the first bad review. As was to be the case throughout the subsequent history of theatre, however, the audience knew what it liked, as did the tyrant Pisistratus, who established competitions for dramatic performances. At the first of these, Thespis was crowned the victor[1]. It is interesting that Solon considered acting dangerous and deceptive. As a lawgiver he was doubtless concerned that the audience might be roused by the performance in ways which could disrupt the peace. Acting was also perceived by him as creating an illusion, convincing the audience of something that was not real. From its known beginnings, therefore, realism, or the illusion of it, was considered to be an essential part of acting.

In the further development of acting in Greece, the poet, who was also usually the actor, introduced further roles, performing them all himself, but distinguishing between them by the use of masks. The poet Aeschylus introduced a second actor and thus made the distinction between poet and actor clear. Sophocles added a third actor and the tradition of employing only three actors who each impersonated several characters by the use of masks with a diminished role for the chorus became established.

The acting in this period was undoubtedly stylised and declamatory. With thousands of people gathered in vast amphitheatres, it was obviously important to enable each member of the audience to see the characters and hear the speeches clearly. Apart from the large masks, big, thick-soled boots, known as a 'cothurnus', were worn, to make the actor seem larger than life. The masks also enabled the actors, all men, to impersonate female roles. For performances in such conditions voice training was obviously crucial. Aristotle wrote of the importance of 'the right management of the voice'[2] for the actor, and the actor Demosthenes stressed the need to be 'splendid in voice'[3]. A good grasp of rhythm and timing was necessary, as was the ability to sing. As the costumes, boots and masks were surely very heavy, gestures and movements must have been slow and demonstrative.

The acting styles within the Greek classical period undoubtedly underwent changes over time, which, in essence, prefigured the cycles of change that occurred in later periods and in other cultures. There is evidence for at least three periods in classical Greece, although the periods cannot be sharply distinguished: that of Aeschylus and Sophocles, in which the acting was very restrained and formal; the fourth century when actors such as Neoptolemus and Theodorus developed a more natural style; and, finally, the plays of Euripides, which introduced a more realistic depiction of human emotion[4]. There were comic actors, too, throughout these periods, who, as with comedians in all ages, developed a freer, often vulgar style.

Rome

The tragedies and comedies developed in Rome were based largely on translations of Greek plays, adapted to Roman contexts. This is true of both the works of the great Roman tragedians, such as Seneca, as well as the comic writers such as Plautus and Terence. The Romans went in for much more spectacular displays than the Greeks, with decorated scenery and also, on occasions, the inclusion of live animals. Most Roman actors had the status of slaves, managed and trained in special troupes, though especially gifted ones could manage to become very wealthy. One such was the renowned Quintus Roscius Gallus (d 62 BC), known generally as Roscius, who eventually gained his freedom and became a personal friend of the writer Cicero. Another actor in the first century, the Greek-born Aesop, was greatly admired for his fiery and emotional performances. A highly declamatory style was most popular with Roman audiences. The Romans did use masks, but it seems that they did not become popular, and the actors were appreciated for their facial expressions and gestures, which seem to have been refined to a highly stylised degree.

The Romans also developed the art of mime to a high degree. A certain Pylades wrote a treatise on mime and founded his own school to put his theories into practice, and many mimes became as famous as the well-known actors of the day.

Roman poets and orators claim to have learned much of their techniques from watching the leading actors, and it is writers such as Cicero (106–43 BC), Quintilian (circa AD 35–95) and Lucian (circa AD 120–200), who have passed on to posterity what accounts are extant of the acting styles of the period. Cicero's *De Oratore* demonstrates this debt. He noted of Roscius 'how everything is done by him unexceptionably; everything with the utmost grace;

everything in such a way as is becoming...'[5] He also stressed the importance of leaving some passages less clear so that others may become the clearer, a point made, in different words, by many modern actors: '...high excellence and merit in speaking should be attended with some portions of shade and obscurity, that the part on which a stronger light is thrown may seem to stand out, and become more prominent...'[6] Lucian, while decrying the decline in acting styles, also has positive advice to give. Writing specifically of pantomime, a term said to have been introduced by Italian Greeks, and of acting in general, he called for verisimilitude: '...prince or tyrannicide, pauper or farmer, each must be shown with the peculiarities that belong to him.'[7] He writes elsewhere of '...the pantomime, whose task it is to identify himself with his subject, and make himself part and parcel of the scene that he enacts.'[8] He also provides a vivid and amusing account of the extremes to which overacting may lead. An actor playing the role of Ajax in a state of madness 'so lost control of himself, that one might have been excused for thinking his madness was something more than feigned'[9]. It appears that the illiterate mass considered it all to be great acting, but the more intelligent part of the audience obviously felt disgust at this display, although they concealed their feelings. Lucian praises another actor, who, in a similar role, 'played it with admirable judgement and discretion, and was complimented on his observance of decorum, and of the proper bounds of his art'[10].

THE MIDDLE AGES

By the fifth and sixth centuries AD, the classical modes of performing tragedy and comedy had degenerated and been changed so much that they were no longer recognisable as such. In Europe as a whole the most popular forms of entertainment were folk dances and various demonstrations of acrobatic skills and juggling. Travelling groups of mimes and conjurors, performing occasionally comic interludes, were common. The nearest they came to acting was in the recitation of narratives about heroic deeds. There was little chance of developing a true histrionic art while the church condemned such groups as disreputable.

Ironically, it was within the church itself that performances of a vaguely theatrical nature were permitted. Simple dramatic structures were developed by the priests chanting Latin dialogue based on stories from the scriptures and these gradually became more complex liturgical dramas. Performances eventually moved from within the church to outside it, with priests being replaced by laymen. By the fourteenth and fifteenth centuries large groups of amateur actors were performing various biblical stories with all members of their communities taking part in the productions in one way or another, building scenery, making props, etc, very much as is still exemplified today in the dramatic festival at Oberammergau. The so-called morality plays became more allegorical and were influenced by the spread of humanism, with the introduction more and more of comic elements and increasingly realistic acting. These changes happened throughout Europe. In France, Spain, Italy and Germany, religious plays were eventually being performed alongside pure farces, with individual writers now becoming well known for their skills in writing comedy, such as the great Hans Sachs in Germany.

Although acting styles were undoubtedly often crude and naïve, with costumes being colourful rather than historically accurate, there were individual performers who acted sensitively and were able to move their audiences. There are documentary accounts of such performances.[11]

There are some writings extant from the Middle Ages which give advice on acting. One in particular recommends a measured, balanced delivery; the actor should clearly avoid excessive emotion. This advice is to be found in the introductory remarks to one of the oldest known French mystery plays, *The Representation of Adam*, written sometime in the twelfth century. Though the dialogue was written in Norman French, the remarks, with suggestions also for costumes, scenery and gestures, were in Latin. The actor playing Adam is given the following advice: 'Adam shall be trained well to speak at the right moment, so that he may come neither too soon nor too late. Not only he, but all shall be well practised in speaking calmly, and making gestures appropriate to the things they say...'[12]

THE SIXTEENTH AND SEVENTEENTH CENTURIES

By the sixteenth and seventeenth centuries, the groups of amateur actors had gradually been superseded by professionals, who replaced the dramas on religious themes with ones of a more secular nature.

England

The Elizabethan period

In 1545, King Henry VIII created the post of Master of the Revels, whose role was to organise the entertainment at his court. For some time, this entertainment consisted of various interludes and elaborate allegorical dramas. At the same time, the popularity of bands of strolling players was growing, groups of professional players under the protection of noblemen, performing on village greens and in the yards of inns.

In the short period of four decades, from about 1580 to 1620, two companies of actors in particular became famed for the quality of their performances: the Admiral's Men, who were run by Philip Henshawe, with the actor Edward Alleyn playing the leading roles in the plays of Christopher Marlowe; and the Lord Chamberlain's Company (known after the accession of James I as the King's Majesty's Servants), with the renowned actors William Kemp and Richard Burbage, and a certain actor and poet called William Shakespeare.

Edward Alleyn was admired especially for his mastery of action on the stage, and it seems he developed a very exaggerated style of acting. Although little is known about how Richard Burbage acted, it seems likely that he exemplified the well-balanced style advocated in Hamlet's advice to the Players. The speech (in Act III, scene II) is too well known to quote it in full, but certain phrases could usefully be emphasised as being crucial to the attainment of a measured style: 'Nor do not saw the air too much with your hand, thus, but use all gently', '...beget a temperance that may give it smoothness', 'Be not too tame neither; but let your own discretion be your tutor. Suit the action to the word, the word to the action; with this special observance, that you o'erstep not the modesty of nature…'

Burbage's well-balanced acting was celebrated in an elegy on his death, which has been attributed to the Earl of Pembroke:

How to ye person hee did suit his face,
How did his speech become him, and his face
Suit with his speech, whilst not a word did fall
Without just weight to balance it withall[13]

Another writer, Richard Flecknoe, who probably never actually saw Burbage act, reported that the actor had the ability to completely immerse himself in his role, 'so wholly transforming himself into his part, and putting off himself with his clothes, as he never (not so much as in the tiring-house) assum'd himself again until the play was done.'[14]

The actor and writer John Webster (d 1634) is likely to have been the author of the essay entitled 'Character of An Excellent Actor'. For Webster, the actor should be at one with nature, and provide living personalities and not just embodiments of moral concepts, 'for what we see him personate, we think truly done before us' and 'what he doth feignedly that do others essentially'.[15]

In general, it seems that acting in the Elizabethan period was likely to have been stylised rather than realistic in any modern sense. The actor was expected to have excellent projection and control of his voice and not overact for the sake of gaining audience approval.

The Restoration and after

During the Civil War, in 1642, London's theatres were closed. The Puritan government kept them closed until 1660 when the restoration of the monarchy occurred with Charles II's return to the throne. In the same year, the king granted patents to Sir William Davenant (1606–1668), a playwright, and his friend Thomas Killigrew (1612–1683) to set up two playhouses and organise two companies of actors, the Duke of York's Company and the King's Men. These two companies dominated the theatrical scene until 1843. Having spent the years of exile in France, the royal court had developed a taste for the French-style of theatrical performance in the classical mode. The old Elizabethan-style playhouse, open to the elements, was replaced by a proscenium-arch stage with a curtain and scenery, though an extensive apron stage was retained. Performances were dominated by the personalities of the leading actors, and the popular plays of the day were very much written to show off their talents. Some outstanding actors did, however, appear who revived interest in great drama.

From 1660 till 1710 the leading actor of his day was Thomas Betterton, who not only took the main roles in the plays of his contemporaries, Etherege, Congreve and Dryden, but also revived Shakespeare's *Hamlet*. For his contemporaries, his acting style was dignified and restrained. He was admired for his ability to express feelings with passion but with a controlled use of his voice. He provided intelligent interpretations and was capable of a large variety of characterisations. During this period, too, many women came to prominence on the stage. Betterton's own wife, Mary Saunders, became the first woman to play the main female roles in Shakespeare's plays.

By 1680 the two companies had built new theatres, the Duke of York's Company in Dorset Gardens, and the King's Men in Drury Lane. In 1682 they united into one company using the Drury Lane theatre.

Italy

Undoubtedly, the form of drama in Italy that had the most lasting effect both on dramatic compositions and acting styles in other European countries, especially on comedy, was the *Commedia dell'Arte*. Originating in the 1560s, it utilised predominantly two techniques of acting: improvisation and stock character types. There was no scenery as such, only a few essential props, and no written scripts, just broad outlines, or 'scenarios', of the general development and outcome of the plot. Playing stock characters with standard traits and personalities, the actors had little freedom for interpretation but could be creative in the improvisation of their own dialogue.

Spain

From the mid-sixteenth century till about 1700, Spain enjoyed what has been termed its Golden Age of literature. Three main types of drama were popular in this period: the *autos sacramentales* (one-act religious plays); *comedias nuevas* (full-length secular plays); and the *zarzuelas*, plays with music. There is an interesting and complex history of how women were at first banned from the stage by the

Catholic Church at this time, with men and boys playing female roles, and then, from about 1600 onwards, allowed on stage but under very strict conditions of supervision. In 1653, a rather quirky law was enacted stipulating that, if required by the text, women could cross-dress as men, but only on the upper half of their bodies[16]. All this is indicative of a very strict moral control of actors' performances in the period, though some bawdy elements doubtlessly crept into the secular comedies. One scholar is of the opinion that performances by Castilian Spanish groups were undoubtedly 'more animated' than those in Italy at the time[17].

It is likely that a more realistic style came into fashion with the production of the plays of the leading dramatist of the latter part of the sixteenth century: Lope de Vega (1562– 1635). He deliberately broke with the three classical unities (of time, place and action), writing in the vernacular and encouraging actors to speak in ways which would communicate with their audiences.

His immediate successor was the man considered by most to be the greatest Spanish dramatist: Pedro Calderón de la Barca. He wrote 80 *autos sacramentales* and 120 *comedias*, as well as many short comic works. If Lope de Vega aimed for a more natural style, Calderón sought a more formal dramatic structure and richness of symbolism, and several of his plays, especially *La vida es sueño* ('Life is a Dream') were to become influential in Europe in the Romantic era. These were not conducive to a natural style of acting.

France

In France, there developed a tradition of many actors adopting a single stage name. One of the first major tragedians of note was known as Mondory (Guillaume Desgilberts, 1594–1651). He established a troupe of actors called the *Théâtre du Marais*. It would seem that he put great vocal and physical exertion into his acting, achieving enormous acclaim for his performances in the plays of Corneille. His fate should be an object lesson, however, to all those actors who are tempted to go well over the top. In one of his performances, the role of King Herod, he exerted himself so much that he had an apoplectic fit which paralysed his tongue. Other well-known actors of the time seem not to have been daunted by Mondory's fate, and the very bombastic and flamboyant style of actors such as Bellerose (Pierre Le Messier) and Montfleury (Zacharie Jacob) became the norm.

The actor and writer who attained the greatest fame in the period and established himself as one of France's great dramatists is undoubtedly Molière (Jean Baptiste Poquelin). In his early years, with his troupe, *L'Illustre Théâtre*, he was greatly influenced by the tradition of Italian comedies. By the 1660s, his troupe had become the most renowned company in the country, especially praised for its ensemble-style acting. As a director, Molière warned his actors constantly against being too unnatural and encouraged them in their efforts to represent characters far removed from their own personalities. His most famous protégé was the great tragedian Michel Baron, who retired in 1691 but returned to the stage as one of its leading exponents of a natural style in 1720.

In 1680, King Louis XIV established the *Théâtre Français*, which, later renamed as the *Comédie Française*, was to become the national theatre company with the longest continuous history in the world. It was run democratically, with its leading actors sharing responsibility for both administration and finance.

Germany

During the sixteenth and seventeenth centuries in Germany there was no established theatre of the kind which already flourished in England, France and Spain. Apart from the itinerant companies continuing the tradition of popular farces, the most common dramatic performances were provided by travelling companies of English, French and Italian players. One man attempted to improve the quality of acting and performance style in the period: Johannes Velten (circa 1640–1693), but little is known about his techniques.

THE EIGHTEENTH CENTURY

England

In the first part of the eighteenth century in England, acting was marked by extremely exaggerated vocal mannerisms. Speeches were delivered with artificially imposed cadences in the current French style. There were many long-drawn-out pauses, and unnatural moves and actions. Associated especially with this period are the actors Colley Cibber and Robert Wilks.

Most of the writing on acting in the period was concerned

to analyse and prescribe formulae for the accomplished actor. The first manual for actors in English is ascribed to Thomas Betterton (first published in 1710). He expressed the wish 'that some men of good sense, and acquainted with the graces of action and speaking, would lay down some rules, by which the young beginners might direct themselves to that perfection, which everybody is sensible is extremely (and perhaps always has been) wanted on our stage... so that from them we might form a system of acting which might be a rule to future players...'[18]

The actor Colley Cibber (1671–1757) had a predilection for an exaggerated style, and it is no surprise therefore to learn that he was the first Lord Foppington, the fop of all fops, in Vanbrugh's *The Relapse*. Yet he appreciated a natural style in others. Of Thomas Betterton's performance as Hamlet he wrote that, unlike many other actors who had presented Hamlet in a violent passion when he encounters his father's ghost for the first time, Betterton 'opened with a pause of mute amazement! Then rising slowly to a solemn, trembling voice, he made the Ghost equally terrible to the spectator as to himself!'[19] For Cibber it was important that the actor identify fully with the feelings of the character being portrayed: 'He that feels not himself the passion he would raise, will talk to a sleeping audience.'[20] While, however, he praised in actors 'a natural freedom, a becoming grace, which is easier to conceive than describe'[21], he also stressed that they must control their voices very much as a singer does: 'The voice of a singer is not more strictly tied to time and tune, than that of an actor in theatrical elocution: the least syllable too long, or too slightly dwelt upon in a period, depreciates it to nothing.'[22]

The actor Charles Macklin (1697?–1797) was the first to attempt to break with the extreme artificiality of the period and introduce something of the quality of normal speech onto the stage. He also encouraged a degree of authenticity in costume by being the first to dress Macbeth in Scottish traditional dress. Another actor and playwright, John Hill, wrote of Macklin:

> It was his manner to check all the cant and cadence of tragedy; he would bid his pupil first speak the passage as he would in common life, if he had occasion to pronounce the same words; and then giving them more force, but preserving the same accent, to deliver them on the stage. Where the player was faulty in his stops or accents, he set them right; and with nothing more than this attention to what was natural, he produced out of the most ignorant persons, players that surprised everybody...[23]

In Macklin's own essay, 'The Art and Duty of an Actor', he wrote: 'The actor must take especial care not to mould and suit the character to his looks, tones, gestures and manners; if he does so, it will become the actor's character, and not the poet's.'[24]

Influenced by Macklin was an actor destined to gain great renown in the history of English theatre: David Garrick. Though he may not have been as naturalistic as Macklin, he did attempt to train those talented actors he gathered around him to develop a more natural style of acting, while being concerned for good posture and graceful movement. He also indulged himself, however, in lengthy, drawn-out emotional scenes, which were apparently very powerful. One of the most precisely detailed and evocative descriptions of his acting can be found in the writings of the German philosopher, scientist and wit Georg Christoph Lichtenberg, who was enthralled by his performance as Hamlet: 'His whole demeanour is so expressive of terror that it made my flesh creep even before he began to speak. The almost terror-struck silence of the audience, which preceded this appearance and filled one with a sense of insecurity, probably did much to enhance this effect.'[25] Lichtenberg provides one of the most precise descriptions of an actor's physical behaviour on the stage, so that it is possible to visualise very clearly the whole sequence of Hamlet's first encounter with the Ghost.

It was Garrick who was responsible for bringing the attention of London audiences to the young actress Sarah Siddons, who managed to combine a naturalness she had learned from Garrick with a certain statuesque quality she had perfected. She also had an emotional depth which endeared her to the new Romantic movement. By contrast, her brother, John Philip Kemble, had a cool, classical and mannered style, which he put to great effect in his most famous role as Coriolanus.

Sarah Siddons was renowned for completely identifying with the role she was playing. Of her performance in the role of Constance in the play *King John* she wrote:

I never, from the beginning of the play to the end of my part in it, once suffered my dressing-room door to be closed, in order that my attention might be constantly fixed on those distressing events, which, by this means, I could plainly hear going on upon the stage... In short, the spirit of the whole drama took possession of my mind and frame, by my attention being incessantly riveted to the passing scenes.[26]

France

Despite Michel Baron's attempt at a comeback with his natural style in 1720, a ponderous declamatory style of tragic acting prevailed throughout eighteenth-century France. The *Comédie Française* continued to present its plays in stunning but historically inaccurate costumes with very self-consciously intoned recitation. There were some attempts to counteract the trend. The actress Adrienne Lecouvreur (1692– 1730), who acted in many productions with Baron, wrote to a friend that the simplicity of her acting was her one merit. When she died, Voltaire wrote of her that she showed 'feeling and truth where formerly had been shown little but artificiality and declamation.'[27]

Voltaire's own influence on acting, however, was in the encouragement of a more fiery emotional style. Two great tragic actresses in particular were moulded by him: Marie-Françoise Dumesmil and Mlle Clairon. Also trained by Voltaire was the actor known as Lekain (Henri Louis Cain, 1728–1778). He was praised for his vocal skills and his ability to use silence to great expressive effect.

One classic work on the nature of acting from this period, still quoted, or at least referred to, is *Le Paradoxe sur le Comédien* of 1773 (usually translated as 'The Paradox of Acting'), by Denis Diderot (1713–1784), who is most famed for his 20 years' work on the establishment of his great encyclopaedia. He was also a playwright and attempted to replace the rather turgid serious drama of his day with plays about ordinary life written in prose rather than verse. His famous essay on acting was written as a reaction to an earlier work, by Pierre Rémond de Sainte-Albine, entitled *Le Comédien* (1747), which had stressed that a high level of sensibility was necessary for good acting. For Diderot, the actor should avoid all sensitivity: 'If the actor were full, really full, of feeling, how could he play the same part twice running with the same spirit and success?'[28] Study and analysis was all-important for him: '...the actor who plays from thought, from study of human nature, from constant imitation of some ideal type, from imagination, from memory, will be one and the same at all performances, will be always at his best mark.'[29]

In the latter part of the eighteenth century there appeared one actor who was revolutionary both in his art and in politics: François Joseph Talma (1763–1826). He spent some years of his youth in London, where he became familiar with a more naturalistic style of acting than was common at the time in France. He also learned to love the works of Shakespeare. Back in France he eventually entered the School of Elocution, which trained the leading actors of the *Comédie Française*. With the help of the comedian Henri Gourgaud Dugazon (1746–1809), he managed to develop a more individual style of acting than was encouraged in the *Comédie Française*. As a minor actor in the company he was unable to introduce many reforms, but he did provide himself with a costume which was reasonably accurate historically when he appeared in Voltaire's *Brutus*. In other productions, too, he took great pains to achieve historical verisimilitude. But, as a republican he and a few others, including Dugazon, were at odds with most members of the company, who were royalists.

Finally, Talma, Dugazon and a few others left the company to start a rival one of their own. In 1791, the National Assembly gave every citizen the right to set up a theatre of their own and perform plays. At last, in the new *Le Théâtre Français de la Rue de Richelieu* (later called simply *Le Théâtre de la République*), Talma was able to start implementing some of the reforms he desired. His company was eventually reunited with the *Comédie Française* in 1799, but in his new theatre. He was highly regarded by Napoleon, who arranged for him to perform in front of the crowned heads of Europe. His life ended sadly because he felt that he had never been able to act in a play which enabled him to fulfil his ideals of natural acting. He complained to Victor Hugo:

> The actor is nothing without a part, and I have never had a real part... that was at once tragic and everyday, at once a king, and a human being... Truth in the plays was unobtainable; I had to be content with putting it into the costumes... No one knows what I might have been if I had found the author I was seeking. As it is, I shall die without once having acted.[30]

Germany

In the early part of the eighteenth century there was a move in Germany towards imitating the highly stylised declamatory style of the contemporary French theatre. The leader of this movement was a writer and academic at the University of Leipzig, Johann Christoph Gottsched (1700–66). His ideas were espoused by the actors Carolina and Johann Neuber. Carolina stressed the importance of thorough rehearsals and introduced very elaborate costumes, but their productions were never popular, with the public clamouring for the ever-popular farces featuring the comic figure of Hanswurst. The great dramatist and theorist Gotthold Ephraim Lessing had his first play staged by the Neubers.

In 1753, Konrad Ekhof (1720–78) made the first attempt to establish a realistic style of acting in Germany by setting up an 'Academy for Actors'. He expressed his philosophy thus: 'Dramatic art is copying nature by art and coming so near up to it that semblance is taken for reality, or to represent things of the past as if they were just happening.'[31] Together with some local citizens, Ekhof also founded the Hamburg National Theatre, with the aim of promoting high-class dramatic productions of works by not only German but also foreign authors. Lessing was appointed the official critic of the theatre and published regular theoretical essays in a periodical sponsored by the theatre. These were finally published as the famous *Hamburg Dramaturgy*. In this, he endeavoured to analyse acting on the basis of Ekhof's natural style of performance, but only a small part of the final work is devoted to this. He was particularly concerned to stress that the actor should understand the meaning of the words and also that he should embody them with his own feelings: 'He must convince us by a firm assured tone of voice that he is penetrated by the full meaning of his words... Yet how far is the actor, who only understands a passage, removed from him who also feels it!'[32]

In the 1770s, the young actor Friedrich Ludwig Schroeder came to the fore. He became essentially an actor-manager, and was the first to perform many of the leading roles in plays by Lessing and Goethe, amongst other important writers. It is reported that he was passionate of nature and revolutionary in spirit. He rejected the artificiality of style associated with the French theatre, and brought to the stage a forceful realism, in, for example *Götz von Berlichingen*, an early play by Goethe in his *Sturm und Drang* period. Between 1776 and 1780 he also produced 11 plays by Shakespeare, and, although he chopped some of them about a bit, his interpretations were considered stunningly realistic. He developed true ensemble acting and a sensitive approach to rehearsing, reading plays through with his company and suggesting possible characterisations. Unlike many actor-managers he was also willing to play minor roles in many of his productions, such as the Ghost in *Hamlet*.

Another actor who gained particular renown in the eighteenth century was August Wilhelm Iffland (1759 –1803). He had trained under Ekhof but came to prominence at the Mannheim National Theatre under the great theatrical entrepreneur Baron Wolfgang Heribert von Dalberg. His fame was based on his own plays as much as his acting. He combined realism with considerable artifice when it suited him, and played the major roles in the first productions of the plays of Friedrich Schiller, who was closely associated with the Mannheim theatre.

The towering presence of Johann Wolfgang von Goethe also made itself felt in the theatre, and not just through his plays. During the period from 1775, when he was the leading cultural figure in the Duchy of Weimar, he not only wrote but also directed and acted in many plays at the Ducal theatre, largely an amateur affair. Eventually, in 1791, he was asked by Duke Karl August, to take over the direction of a newly built theatre with professional actors. For 26 years he reigned supreme in this small theatrical world. In his mature years, his aesthetic ideals were those of classical beauty of form and harmony. He attempted to improve the acting style of his company with a set of 'Rules for Actors'. These were far removed from the principles followed by Schroeder, and stressed formal posture, gestures and precise pronunciation, avoiding all distortions by dialects. Schiller's arrival in Weimar complemented Goethe's restrained style with greater liveliness.

Acting throughout the eighteenth century in Germany thus came to be dominated by the polarity of Hamburg realism and Weimar classicism. Signs of the Romanticism to come are evidenced in the fiery acting style of Johann Friedrich Ferdinand Fleck (1757–1801) at the Royal Court Theatre in Berlin. Fleck was the first to play the role of Wallenstein in Schiller's great trilogy.

Russia

Steps were already being taken in eighteenth-century Russia to establish a more professional theatre. The tragic actor Ivan Dmitrevsky (1734–1821) went to observe French and English drama at first hand, meeting and discussing with David Garrick. He was appointed by Catherine the Great to the directorship of the first theatrical school in the country. His stated aims were not only to encourage actors to be more creative in their performances but also to develop an awareness of the links between their art and their country; to lend, in other words, a national identity to drama. The playwright Peter Plavilshchikov (1760–1812) was also concerned to use his art to the end of establishing a sense of national identity. He wanted a style of drama which was akin to the character of the Russian people: 'The Russians demand not words, but deeds; they desire little to be said, but much to be implied; they love the intricate, but cannot endure the excessively sweet; love order and will not suffer pedantry.'[33]

THE NINETEENTH CENTURY

England

Despite the attempts undertaken in the eighteenth century, by such actors as Macklin and Garrick, to introduce greater naturalism into the theatre, the style of most performances remained high-flown and artificial with standardised gestures. In the nineteenth century, however, theatrical tastes gradually changed. More middle- and upper-class people were going to the theatre, and a politer, more genteel style of play and performance was appreciated. The proscenium stage became the norm, with boxed sets imitating scenes from real life.

The early years of the century were still dominated by the acting styles of Sarah Siddons and her brother John Philip Kemble, but, with the advent of Edmund Kean in 1814, a more Romantic style came to prevail.

To the poet Coleridge is attributed the much-quoted comment: 'To see Kean was to read Shakespeare by flashes of lightning.'[34] And Byron noted in his diary: 'Just returned from seeing Kean in *Richard*. By Jove, he is a soul! Life, nature, truth without exaggeration or diminution.'[35] Leigh Hunt, the Romantic critic, commented that Kean seemed to actually know the passion he invoked: 'Kean knows the real thing, which is the height of the *passion*, manner following it as a matter of course, *and grace being developed from it in proportion to the truth of the sensation...*'[36] For the critic William Hazlitt, Kean's acting had 'the stamp and freshness of nature', and he wrote: 'He is possessed with a fury, a demon that leaves him no repose, no time for thought or room for imagination.'[37] Kean's responses to such views of him are enlightening and have a ring of truth that doubtless applies to all good acting. He complained to the widow of Garrick that the critics were mistaken:

These people don't understand their business; they give me credit where I don't deserve it, and pass over the passages on which I have bestowed the utmost care and attention. Because my style is easy and natural they think I don't study, and talk about the 'sudden impulse of genius'. There is no such thing as impulsive acting; all is premeditated and studied beforehand. A man may act better or worse on a particular night, from particular circumstances; but although the execution may not be so brilliant, the conception is the same.[38]

Another giant of the nineteenth century was William Charles Macready. Critics of the time noted that he reminded them of Kemble, but in speech and gesture seemed to have borrowed much from Kean. Distinctive about his style was his preference for introducing small, everyday details into highly tragic sequences. Hazlitt wrote: 'Mr Macready, sometimes, to express uneasiness and agitation, composes his cravat, as he would in a drawing-room. This is, we think, neither graceful nor natural in extraordinary situations.'[39] It was, however, indicative of the growing taste for realism in the theatre.

The dramatist, director and actor Tom Robertson did much to hasten the development towards a more realistic style, together with the actors Marie Wilton Bancroft and Squire Bancroft. The actor John Hare (1844–1921) wrote of Robertson: 'As nature was the basis of his own work, so he sought to make actors understand it should be theirs. He thus founded a school of Natural acting which completely revolutionised the then existing methods, and by so doing did incalculable good to the stage.'[40]

The last decades of the nineteenth century were dominated by the names of the great actor-managers: Sir Henry Irving, Sir Herbert Beerbohm Tree and Sir George Alexander. Irving was renowned for his idiosyncratic playing of the major Shakespeare roles and in contemporary melodramas. They somehow managed to blend the styles of Kean and Macready with at least some superficial trappings of a Robertson-style naturalism.

The socially and psychologically profound and disturbing plays of Ibsen were beginning to be introduced, though George Bernard Shaw, in his championing of Ibsen, found that the contemporary English theatre was not equipped to do justice to his plays. Jacob Thomas Grein (1862–1935) did mount a production of *Ghosts* in 1891, however, and with this set up his Independent Theatre, in which he also produced Shaw's first play, *Widowers' Houses*. The company collapsed in 1897, but it inspired the setting up of many other experimental theatres devoted to the new realism.

Shaw had much to say about acting, in the familiar, forceful, arrogant style he applied to almost everything he wrote. Sir Henry Irving he dismissed for his 'hackneyed stage tricks'[41]. Of Beerbohm Tree he wrote that he 'felt that he needed nothing from an author but a literary scaffold on which to exhibit his own creations'[42]. He stressed that technical accomplishments alone do not make an actor: 'By themselves they will no more make an actor than grammar and spelling will make an author, or fingering and blowing a bandsman...'[43]

France

The Romantic movement in France, despite the notorious opening night in 1830 of Victor Hugo's *Hernani*, with its bevy of oddly dressed poets, did little to change the theatre scene. Most popular at the time were the prose comedies and dramas of Eugène Scribe. In Scribe's play *Adrienne Lecouvreur* the actress Rachel (Eliza Felix, 1821–58) made her name. She had been a poor street singer and came to dominate the stage of the *Comédie Française* over next 15 years. She had excellent diction and a graceful presence. Although she wrote no account of her method of preparing a role, it would seem from the words she is reported to have uttered on her deathbed that she had no time for artifice and needed to understand and identify fully with her role: 'In studying for the stage, take my word for it, declamation and gesture are of little avail. You have to think and weep.'[44]

A leading actor in the second half of the nineteenth century was Benoit Constant Coquelin (1841–1909). He resigned from the then *Théâtre Français* in 1886 and went on tour in Europe and to America. Eventually, in 1892, he set up a company of his own. His particular forte was the classic comic roles, though he also played serious roles in contemporary plays. He has left a precise description of how he built up a role, which should not be unfamiliar to modern actors:

> When I have to create a new role, I begin by reading the play with the greatest attention, five or six times. First, I consider what position my character should occupy, on what plan in the picture I must put him. Then I study his psychology, knowing what he thinks and what he is morally. I deduce what he ought to be physically, what will be his carriage, his manner of speaking, his gesture. These characteristics once decided, I learn the part without thinking about it further. Then, when I know it, I take up my man again, and closing my eyes I say to him, 'Recite this for me.'[45]

From the 1860s till the outbreak of World War I Sarah Bernhardt dominated the French stage with her great beauty and carefully calculated effects. Bernard Shaw wrote that her acting was 'not the art of making you think more highly or feel more deeply, but the art of making you admire her'. He wrote also: 'She does not enter into the leading character, she substitutes herself for it.'[46] Her lack of concern for realism was evidenced supremely by her appearance on stage at the age of 71 after having had one of her legs amputated. Ironically, in her book *The Art of the Theatre* she stresses the importance of naturalism and adds: 'Fidelity to the truth does not always distinguish in our present-day art, and the public will not tolerate a glossing over of reality.'[47]

Some mention must be made of François Delsarte (1811–71), if only because he was to become influential in America, via so-called 'Delsarte recitation books', and was referred to, albeit critically, by the leading exponent of the Method school of acting, Lee Strasberg. Delsarte attempted to formulate strict laws of speech and gesture and Strasberg wrote of him:

> In the nineteenth century the Frenchman Delsarte becomes dissatisfied with the routine acting techniques taught in his time. Aware of its mechanical and stultifying character, he grows to realise that under the stress of natural instinct or emotion the body takes on the appropriate attitude or gesture, and this gesture was not at all what his teachers taught it was. But unable or unwilling to rely on what he had discovered he tried to create a new series of elaborate pictorial descriptions that ended by being just as mechanical as those he originally broke away from.[48]

At the turn of the century, André Antoine established the first successful experimental theatre in France, the *Théâtre Libre*, which rejected all that the *Comédie Française* stood for, and introduced the kind of naturalism suitable to the plays of Zola and Hauptmann. It was also his deliberate policy to use untrained amateur actors.

Germany and Austria

In the early nineteenth century, an actor came to the fore in Germany who was well suited to the moody, psychologically complex roles in the new Romantic drama. The style of acting of Ludwig Devrient was generally considered to be emotionally uninhibited. His first great success was as Karl Moor in Schiller's *The Robbers*. So much did he exert himself in his performances that, on one occasion, he could not complete a performance of *King Lear*. The excessive emotionalism of his acting and his passion for drinking caused his career to be short-lived. The Devrient family also spawned other men of the theatre. Two of Ludwig's nephews, Karl August and Gustave Emil, became leading tragedians, and Eduard, another nephew, became director of the *Hoftheater*, Dresden, and then of the *Karlsruhe Theater*. Between 1848 and 1874 he published a huge five-volume study of the history of acting in Germany: *Geschichte der Deutschen Schauspielkunst*. In this he advocated a natural style of acting as opposed to the style practised at Weimar, which he condemned as antiquated and pretentious. He himself had also acted and he described his approach thus: 'I have always yielded to the impression which the nature of the role has evoked in me; I have always tried to give what I have seen and inwardly felt in the part. Never have I thought out or devised particular nuances in order to highlight a specific point.'[49]

Generally regarded as one of the finest theatres in Europe in the nineteenth century was the *Burgtheater* in Vienna, Austria. The dramatist, Heinrich Laube, who had been associated with the politically left-wing 'Young Germany' movement for a while, was its director from 1849 until

1866. Laube became renowned for being one of the first directors to prepare very precise instructions for each of his productions. The theatre clearly combined all that was best in acting techniques in the period because it became the ultimate goal of all German-speaking actors to act in the *Burgtheater*. In an article on the Thimig family of actors Maria Darnton wrote: 'To be a member of the *Burgtheater* was in those days the dream of every German-speaking actor. The fountainhead of histrionic tradition, exigent in technical standards, unrivalled in range and variety of repertory, the names of some of its greatest actors… have transcended the limits of language…'[50]

In the second half of the century, one particular German troupe, the Meiningen Company, was to have international influence. It was established by the Duke Georg II of Saxe-Meiningen (1826–1914), who encouraged ensemble acting and historical accuracy in all aspects of the productions. Much time and attention were given to thorough rehearsals. The company performed in all the major capitals of Europe and influenced specifically the founder of the French *Théâtre Libre*, André Antoine, who admired their handling of crowd scenes, and the leading Russian theorist Stanislavsky, who was eventually, however, to criticise the Meiningen approach, especially for the disciplinarian methods of its stage manager, Ludwig Chronegk, the type of director 'who made the actor a stage property on the same level with stage furniture, a pawn that was moved about in their *mise-en-scène*…'[51] Thus, while the Meiningen Company encouraged better ensemble acting, it also paved the way for the dominance of the *Regisseur* (from the French '*régisseur*') in the German theatre.

As in France, the end of the century saw the advent of naturalism in the theatre, with the *Freie Bühne* in Berlin being directly influenced by the *Théâtre Libre* and realising the naturalist ideals of its leading light Otto Brahm – the main difference being that the *Freie Bühne* was able to use a fully equipped theatre and professional actors. This theatre in its turn inspired the setting up of the *Freie Volksbühne*, which aimed to provide realistic drama for the working classes under the slogan 'Art for the People'.

Russia

In the early nineteenth century the Russian tragedian Pavel Mochalov (1800–48) became famous for his performances of Shakespearean heroes, especially Hamlet, very much in the fiery Romantic style. He wrote: 'Spiritual profundity and a flaming imagination are two qualities which form the main components of talent', adding: 'Only when an actor has the ability to imagine what he himself is living with the mind and soul of the audience, that is, when he can force the audience to share his joy and tears, force his imagination vividly to conjure up the scene; in a word, only when the actor feels keenly his position, then for a moment, can he force the audience to forget itself.'[52]

There are traceable links between the early theorist of stage realism, Michael Shchepkin (1788–1863), and the Stanislavsky school. Shchepkin insisted on having actors justify every detail of their performance and every gesture, which had to be rooted in a psychological understanding of the character. To the actor SV Shumsky he offered the following advice:

Do not reject criticism, but search for its deeper meaning, and in order to test yourself and the criticism, always keep in mind – nature: crawl under the skin of your character, so to speak, study well his particular ideas, if there are any, and do not even exclude from consideration the social influences of his past. Then, no matter what situations are taken from life, you will always express them truthfully: you may sometimes play poorly, sometimes only satisfactorily (that often depends on your own inner disposition), but you will always play truthfully.[53]

The playwright and director Alexander Nikolayevich Ostrovsky appealed to Czar Alexander III to establish an inexpensive theatre with drama for the people, and based on ensemble acting. He was eventually to found the Russian Academy of Dramatic Art.

In 1898 Konstantin S Stanislavsky (1863–1938) created a theatre, together with the playwright Vladimir I Nemirovich-Danchenko, in which they planned to produce carefully rehearsed, naturalistic performances of both Russian and foreign plays. It became famous for the first successful productions of the dramatist Anton Chekhov. Stanislavsky's writings were the first and are still the most extensive body of theory about the nature of acting and they span the last decades of the nineteenth century and the first four decades of the twentieth century. His ideas were rooted in his experiences of nineteenth-century acting styles but his influence was to be most pervasive in the twentieth century. It makes for greater coherence, therefore, if his ideas are considered at the beginning of the section on the twentieth century.

America

In the period after the War of Independence, many American drama companies began to entice English actors over to perform in the classic Shakespearean roles. From the beginning of the nineteenth century these English actors tended to dominate the scene, some of them staying on to work in America permanently. Many other famous names went there on tour, such as Macready, Kean, Charles and Fanny Kemble, etc.

The native-born James Henry Hackett (1800–71) became famous as Falstaff and was the original Rip Van Winkle. Edwin Forrest became the first real native star of the theatre and appeared in many roles especially written for him, as well as playing the leads in *Macbeth*, *King Lear* and *Othello*. His style of acting was greatly influenced by Edmund Kean, and he would tend to adopt statuesque poses and speak in a declamatory style. He became the standard against which, for a long time, all other American actors were measured.

The first great American actress, Charlotte Cushing (1816–76), styled herself closely on the English actress Sarah Siddons.

By the 1850s, a more naturalistic style began to appear, especially as evidenced in the portrayal of Hamlet by Edwin Booth. Another actor in this vein was Joseph Jefferson who was described as acting with good taste and restraint, combined with a capacity for great tenderness and pathos. Louisa Lane Drew took over the management of the Arch Street Theatre, Philadelphia in 1861 and established a stock company with the best actors of the period. Another influential company was Augustin Daly's Company which could boast the English actor Maurice Barrymore, who married Louisa Lane Drew's daughter Georgianna. They produced a renowned family of actors: Lionel, Ethel and John.

By the end of the century, although a realistic style of acting was common, a precursor of the star system was dominant, and audiences tended to be attracted by star names rather than other qualities of the productions. Repertory companies had given way to the production of commercially successful plays in New York which were then sent on tours in so-called road companies. Control of theatre companies was gradually transferred from actor-managers to businessmen, and the concept of 'show business' was born.

Italy

One phenomenon of the dramatic scene in nineteenth-century Italy should not be overlooked, attaining as it did a role of international influence: that of the actress Eleonora Duse (1858–1924).

She was born into a theatrical family and started acting at the age of four, becoming famous later in roles which had also been performed by Sarah Bernhardt. She eventually toured many countries in Europe, Russia, America and South America, and is mainly remembered for her performances in the plays of Henrik Ibsen and Gabriele d'Annunzio. She was a much more introverted person than Bernhardt, and was preferred as an actress by George Bernard Shaw, who saw them both. She developed a role by what she termed 'elimination of the self', allowing what she conceived to be the inner sufferings and joys of the character to take over her own personality. She also argued famously that the theatre as it existed in her time should die. It was suffocating. It should return to something akin to the Greek open-air theatre.

THE TWENTIETH CENTURY AND ITS LEGACY

England

At the turn of the century, there was a movement against the prevailing trend towards naturalism, exemplified most notably by the work of Gordon Craig, son of the renowned actress Ellen Terry. In his work *The Art of the Theatre* he called for a theatre liberated from the obsession with realism: theatre should be poetic and imaginative. He was much admired and designed productions for Eleonora Duse, Otto Brahm in Germany and for the Moscow Arts Theatre. He also sought greater creative freedom for the actor. In an essay entitled 'Theatre Advancing' he wrote, 'I ask only for the liberation of the actor that he may develop his own powers and cease from being the marionette of the playwright.'[54] The Irish poet William Butler Yeats was greatly influenced by his ideas. In 1898, Yeats founded the Irish Literary Theatre, hoping to provide a theatre for Ireland which would be devoted not to the new naturalism but to poetry. He worked closely with the famous Abbey Theatre in Dublin for a while, but his ideals of developing a poetic quality to dramatic speech clashed with the realist ideals which eventually prevailed there.

The actors William and Frank Fay were also closely

associated with the Abbey Theatre. In his work *Merely Players* William wrote:

> The actor must use his own individuality and personality as the medium through which he displays the various thoughts, emotions and actions that constitute the character the dramatist has given him to play. The extent to which he can make his audience believe in its reality is the measure of his professional ability. The audience should feel that everything that happens before them on the stage is as natural to the actor as eating his dinner, or brushing his hair. This natural acting can only be acquired by completely mastering technique and then only using as much of that knowledge as is necessary 'to put the part over.[55]

In the rest of the twentieth century, acting styles in England, as elsewhere, became very diversified and eclectic, although changing preferences can be traced through the decades: what was perceived by one generation as realistic is seen by the next as mannered; and the frankness of one age is the coyness of the next. In the early part of the century most actors gained their experience through independent commercial theatres and repertory companies; in the latter part – and this has continued into the twenty-first century – most underwent some sort of formal training in special drama schools. The advent of the cinema has meant not only that more precise analysis of the changing styles of acting has become possible, but also a whole new technique has become necessary, and the same has become true for television acting.

Many of the actors who have expressed themselves most interestingly on the art of acting in the first half of the twentieth century are either still alive or have only died quite recently. As many of the actors and actresses cited in the second half of the present book quote and refer to such respected actors frequently and often from personal acquaintance, such leading exponents will be considered in detail in that context.

France

In the early twentieth century there was in France, as in England, a reaction against naturalism by some. In particular, the writer and critic Jacques Copeau was concerned to restore a sense of beauty to the theatre. This he achieved by stressing the importance of physical exercise and dance. Others, such as Gaston Baty, came under the influence of Russian and German producers and attempted to establish a system in which the actors became more like pawns under the supreme artistic control of stage managers. Jean Cocteau developed a more stylised drama, also evidenced in his films, which incorporated surrealist elements. A leading light throughout the first part of the century was Jean-Louis Barrault, who blended very successfully subtle verbal skills with imaginative use of mime. He wrote: 'Mime and diction are the two sides of an actor's art, and the visual and auditory sensations must crystallise into a unity for the actor as well as for the audience.'[56]

As with other countries, a large proportion of the good dramatic art which France has given the world during the twentieth century and after has been cinematic.

Germany

The first notable genius of theatrical production to come to the fore in Germany in the early twentieth century and also to eventually establish for himself an international reputation was Max Reinhardt. He was trained as an actor in the naturalistic style by Otto Brahm, but became famous for his unique and idiosyncratic productions, often on a mammoth scale, utilising huge auditoria and arenas. Many of the greatest names in German drama of the time were at some point associated with his productions: Albert Bassermann, Conrad Veidt, Emil Jannings, Paul Wegener, Werner Krauss, Oscar Homolka, Elizabeth Bergner, etc. He was also among the first, between 1917 and 1920, to stage plays in the new Expressionist style, which required exaggerated sets, with distorted angles and brash colours, and the emotive projection of profound human conflicts through an acting style utilising very formal gestures. In the words of one of the movement's leading exponents, Walter Hasenclever: 'Reality on the stage is of no account; all the persons in the play have only to reflect the Ego of the poet as set down in the principal character.'[57]

Very much influenced by the style of Expressionist drama, though not its ideology, were the theatrical productions of Erwin Piscator and Bertolt Brecht. They used deliberately non-naturalist techniques to convey forcefully specific political ideals. Brecht, especially, developed, in his own theoretical writings, a concept of epic theatre, which required a totally different style of acting to that practised hitherto. Audiences were not to be drawn into emotional identification with the characters on stage but should reflect critically upon them and their plights. Thus, while his actors were to use declamation and highly stylised forms of movement and gesture, the purpose was not to heighten the emotional force of the performances but to make audiences aware of the unreality of them, as they would be in observing caricatures, and to provoke the audience through the ironies perceived into thinking critically along specific political, namely left-wing socialist, lines. Communist ideals are often hinted at if not openly stated. Accordingly, therefore, the actor should not attempt to become the character he or she is playing but, as far as possible, stand outside it, revealing through irony the paradoxes and illusions in the personality depicted. It should be as though he or she were commenting on the character for the sake of the audience: understanding should replace identification.

In the early German cinema, some of the styles of Expressionist and epic acting have been preserved, as have the attempts to return to a more realistic style, in, for example, the films in the 1930s by GW Pabst. With the advent of National Socialism, grand emotive gesturing and the encouragement of identification with heroic figures was in again, in support, this time, of an extreme right-wing ideology. Since the Second World War acting styles in Germany have become as eclectic as elsewhere in Europe and the Americas.

Italy

A notable innovator in the twentieth-century Italian theatre was Dario Fo, a renowned playwright, theatre director, actor and composer, who received the Nobel Prize for Literature in

1997. He has consciously delved back into the comic style of the *Commedia dell'Arte*. He has never hesitated to handle politically sensitive topics. He and his wife, Franca Rame, founded the theatre collective *Associazione Nuova Scena* in 1968 which provided drama productions easily adaptable for touring. A particular influence on many young actors was his play *Mistero Buffo* (meaning 'Comic Mystery') in 1969, which was based on medieval plays but dealt with topical issues. It consisted of a sequence of monologues, with the stress on narrative rather than playing roles, that in Italy is known as *teatro di narrazione*. There are no individual dramatic characters, and it has much more in common with age-old techniques of storytelling, thus nourishing modern theatre by reaching back to its roots. In 1970, Fo and his wife left *Nuova Scena* over political differences with other members of the group, and set up another theatre collective: *Colletivo Teatrale La Commune*. It produced plays based on improvisation sessions with the actors, culminating in the now internationally famous *Accidental Death of an Anarchist* (1970). His experimental acting, rehearsing and production styles, as well as his committed political ideology, have inspired many kinds of satirical theatre groups throughout the world.

Russia

Stanislavsky and Nemirovich-Danchenko (see also previous section on Russian acting in the nineteenth century) were responsible for the first successful production of Chekhov's *The Seagull* at the Moscow Arts Theatre. It was established very much as an actors' theatre. The actor was paramount in the creative process. In the words of Nemirovich-Danchenko: 'The director should become lost in the creative process of the actor.'[58] Actors should explore both the role and themselves in depth in order to be able to embody the character.

Stanislavsky developed his ideas on the art of acting at great length, and he outlined what came to be known as his 'system' most clearly in two books, *An Actor Prepares* and *My Life in Art*. He did not manage to complete his planned comprehensive study of the art of acting but there are 12,000 manuscripts extant. His principles were essentially nothing fundamentally new. As can be seen from the earlier accounts of the acting of great naturalist actors of the past, his principles are basically those employed by almost all good actors, but he was not content to leave good performances to chance and intuition.

He wanted to develop a technique of creating conditions in which each actor could easily find the inspiration to perform his or her role well. The American director Lee Strasberg, closely associated with the so-called Method school, has summarised Stanislavsky's system thus: 'It tries to analyse why an actor is good one night and bad another, and therefore to understand what actually happens when an actor acts.' A little later he adds: 'It teaches not how to play this or that part but how to create organically.'[59]

For Stanislavsky, the actor should endeavour to train the medium he or she must use, which is the human body. The body must be controlled but also able to relax so that the actor may concentrate on the performance. One concept about which there have been many differences of opinion is what Stanislavsky described as an imaginary 'circle' surrounding the actor: the actor should imagine the existence of a circle around him or her, excluding all extraneous influences and disturbances, so that concentration will not be disrupted. It has been argued that thinking in this way isolates the actor from other actors and from the audience and leads to excessive self-absorption – though, to be fair to Stanislavsky, he did also stress the importance of understanding the logic of the interactions with other characters in the play.

All actors had to undertake extensive study of the play and their roles in it, exploring the various implied meanings at all levels, the 'sub-text', and also investigate the historical context of the play thoroughly. In building up their own roles they had to ask themselves constantly what actions they were undertaking in each sequence, why they were acting so, and how this action should be best accomplished.

It was also necessary for actors to believe in the truth of what they were doing: 'The actor must first of all believe in everything that takes place on the stage, and most of all must believe in what he himself is doing. And one can believe only in the truth.'[60] It is essentially the notion of make-believe, or what Stanislavsky preferred to call the creative 'if'. The actor should say to him or herself: 'All these properties, make-ups, costumes, the scenery, the publicness of the performance, are lies. I know they are lies, I know I do not need any of them. But *if* they were true, then I would do this and this, and I would behave in this manner and this way towards this and this event.'[61]

Stanislavsky and Nemirovich-Danchenko did not, however, reign supreme in Russian theatre early in the twentieth century. There were, as ever, reactions against naturalism. At the opposite pole and very much in the mould of the *régisseur* was Vsevolod Meyerhold. He sought to involve the minds of his audience in the performance by meaningful symbolic aspects of the production: this required inevitably stylised sets and gestures, and generally a very formal and artificial mode of acting. The inspirations for his symbols and modes of presentation came from many and varied sources: medieval drama, the *Commedia dell'Arte* and the Japanese Kabuki theatre. As his theatrical vision became more and more extreme, he finally fell foul of the government and his group was closed down.

Another actor-producer in a similar mould to Meyerhold was Alexander Tairov, who, together with his wife, founded the Kamerny Theatre (its name meaning 'chamber theatre') in 1914. They completely controlled all aspects of the productions, imposing artificially intoned delivery of the text and stylised gestures.

Other directors attempted to develop a theatrical style which blended the naturalism of Stanislavsky and the extreme artificiality of the likes of Meyerhold. Eugene Vakhtangov, for one, wanted to reveal the eternal and symbolic in contemporary reality: 'Not everything of the times is eternal, but the eternal is always of the times... one should be able to feel today in tomorrow and tomorrow in today.'[62]

Nikolai Okhlopkov attempted to blend the two extremes through the development of mass drama, using bare spaces with movable platforms. Actors and audiences came into close proximity with each other. The writer André van Gyseghem reported of an Okhlopkov production: 'Such proximity disciplines the actor, leads him to "fine" acting with something of the quality of a water-colour, stimulates him to strive for unusual exactness in his emotional expression.'[63]

Finally, it should be mentioned that the approach to acting of the Stanislavsky school greatly influenced film acting in Russia, and especially the theories about film acting developed by Vsevolod Pudovkin and Sergei Eisenstein. In his work *The Film Sense* Eisenstein wrote that 'the lifelike acting of an actor is built, not on his representing the copied results of feelings, but on his causing the feelings to *arise, develop, grow into other feelings – to live before the spectator.*'[64]

Poland

One unique contribution to drama and acting theory in the twentieth century is that of the Polish theatre director Jerzy Grotowski. Justice cannot be done to the complex development of his work and ideas in the present context. Only a few implications for the work of the actor can be indicated.

After graduating with a degree in acting from Kraków in 1954 he went to study directing at the Lunarcharsky Institute of Theatre Arts in Moscow. Here he became familiar with the ideas of Stanislavsky, Vakhtangov, Meyerhold and others. From the late-1950s, he undertook his own productions in Poland. He developed a notion which he called 'poor theatre'. For him, theatre should not try to compete with television and film especially. 'Poor' meant stripping the theatre of all that was not essential: the sets, make-up, costumes, lighting, special effects, etc. In one of his productions, *The Tragical History of Doctor Faustus*, in 1964, all props and objects on the stage were represented by the actors' own bodies, so that in one scene, for example, when the pope is seated at dinner, one actor played his chair and another the meal he was eating. All-important were the actors' intimate encounters with the audience, the direct human communication. What the actor could do with body and voice alone became paramount, inviting the audience to commune with the actor and thereby understand. It is not surprising, therefore, that he came to regard the actor as being in a sacred space, functioning almost like a priest, and that the theatrical experience should become for the audience akin to participating in the Catholic mass.

Greatly influenced by Grotowski have been the British director and drama theorist Peter Brook and the American directors Andre Gregory and James Slowiak, amongst others.

America

At the beginning of the twentieth century the major theatres in America were dominated by commercial interests. Some small companies did try, however, to follow the leads of the new naturalistic and experimental drama developing in Europe. In the period before the First World War, many small, idealistic theatrical groups appeared. Many of these small groups joined together in 1919 to form the Theatre Guild, with the aim of combining the ideals of a good repertory company with commercial success. It had its own school and a subscription audience. It was concerned to produce the best of the new experimental European drama, by writers such as Shaw, Strindberg and the German Expressionist Ernst Toller, alongside the works of exciting new American writers such as Elmer Rice, Maxwell Anderson, Eugene O'Neill, and others. The Theatre Guild did not hold to any firm tenets regarding acting and production style, but it was particularly interested in the development of ensemble work and a realistic style of acting. Amongst other well-known names, it nurtured the talents of Alfred Lunt, Lynn Fontanne and Edward G Robinson.

Serious attention to the art of acting came with the growing concern in the 1930s for theatre to reflect and affect the social ills of the times. In the period of extensive economic depression many of the drama groups, including the Group Theatre, the Theatre Union and others, became concerned to use drama in the fight for political and economic change. In 1931, Lee Strasberg and others from the original Theatre Guild founded the Group Theatre, with the aim of producing contemporary plays with social relevance and following the example of the Russian Eugene Vakhtangov, who attempted to blend naturalism with symbolism. The Group Theatre also aimed to establish a permanent company of actors following the models of the Moscow Arts Theatre and the Abbey Theatre in Ireland. The training of actors was to proceed according to Stanislavsky's methods. The venture lasted for about a decade and managed to produce many actors who were to become internationally known through the medium of film, such as John Garfield, Franchot Tone, Elia Kazan, Lee J Cobb and Clifford Odets, who also established himself as a leading dramatist.

It is worth clarifying here the phrases the 'Method' and the 'Method School', which many actors on both sides of the Atlantic are wont to refer to. These concepts refer to the particular mode of actor training employed by a number of acting schools in America and adapted from the ideas of Stanislavsky.

Other effective drama ventures of the thirties were the New Theatre League, a loosely organised network of non-professional groups which focused on producing drama in unconventional locations where they could reach workers and the unemployed directly, and the Federal Theatre, which was concerned primarily with making sure that actors, directors and theatre crews in general could acquire employment. Acting styles were developed appropriate to the expressive needs of the moment.

Some mention must be made of Michael Chekhov, whom it is difficult to fit into a history of acting organised by nationality, although he did spend an especially influential period of his life in America. He was a nephew of Anton Chekhov and was both influenced by, as well as reacting against, aspects of the theories of Stanislavsky. He went to America in the late 1920s, where he set up his own studio. From 1930 to 1939, he worked in the Kaunas State Theatre in Lithuania; in 1936 he established the Chekhov Theatre School at Dartington Hall, in Devon, England, where he worked until 1939, at which point he moved back to America, where he set up his school again in Connecticut. His approach was very much focused on the inner life of the actor. Much was made of accessing the unconscious creative self through various physical means rather than analysis. He wrote several books about his life as an actor, including *On the Technique of Acting* (1942), and also acted in several films.

Perhaps more than in most other countries, styles of acting in America have been greatly influenced by the rapid growth of the film industry and, at a later stage, of television drama. As elsewhere, too, styles of acting have become as varied as the requirements of producers and directors. Many of the actors, of both stage and screen, quoted in the latter half of this book, often reveal awareness of differences between American and British styles of acting in particular, very much to the detriment of the Americans in general. While many American actors are greatly respected for their abilities, it would seem that the overall concern for slick, well-made and highly commercial products, both for the cinema and television, and the continuing dominance of the star system, have produced acting styles and forms of characterisation which many actors find unsatisfying compared with the possibilities still to be found only in the live theatre.

MASTERING THE ART

THE ACTING EXPERIENCE

Being an actor is, compared with most other professions, except perhaps that of the dramatist and the novelist, a very remarkable way of existing. Actors spend their time developing and being other selves. Many of us pretend, at times, to have qualities and to be in moods with which we do not actually identify ourselves, but we rarely do so for the sake of the pretence alone, and usually have some ulterior motives. Actors have the ability to let go of their own selves, to subsume them under other selves which they, in collaboration with dramatist and director, have invented. Outside the realm of theatre or film such behaviour would be regarded as psychotic. It is only considered acceptable in the play of children or childlike people. It should not be surprising, therefore, to discover that, in actors' own reports about their experiences of acting and becoming an actor, there is evidence of the persistence of elements of childhood play into adulthood, as well as a certain instability with regard to their own identity. Many speak of having felt, from a very early age, the need and ability to perform in some way. This has led many to claim that an actor is indeed born and not made. Whatever the truth of the matter, it does seem to be the case that most actors have felt an inclination to act or show off and play with words right from the start. Once the inclination is discovered there is some hope that the ability may be nurtured.

Annabel Arden, actress and director of plays and operas, has said that acting is a basic form of human behaviour common to us all, and, in its purest form, it is play. She cites the example of a young child picking up a crumb from a table. The child directs all its energy towards picking up the crumb. She believes that actors need to bring such a degree of presence and concentration to their performances.[65] Simon Callow, stage and film actor, director, and author of several books on acting and actors, also considers acting to be an activity which is 'deeply and seriously childish'. He writes that actors revert to a period in their lives in which their personalities are undetermined and in a condition of flux. Like children in play, they are always trying things out and imitating others. He concludes his thoughts on this topic with the words: 'It's neither comfortable nor easy to get hold of your child-self again, but it's behind all great acting and all great theatre.'[66] It's easy to act when you are a child, but it becomes more difficult for most people as they get older. Peter Barkworth, theatre and television actor, writer and teacher, has also stressed that actors start in childhood, but that, as most people grow up, they become shy and self-conscious.[67]

Being unable 'to get hold of your child-self again' would seem to be the condition of those adults who could not act to save their lives. An incapacity to act is clearly related to an inability to let go of their adult selves. This is a polite way of saying that they are too concerned about their own dignity and the respect of others to be willing to indulge publicly in childish behaviour. An adult person who behaves persistently like a child is considered to be a fool. To be an actor you have to be willing to make a fool of yourself.

The actress Ayşan Çelik, educated and acting in America, has spoken of her experience of exercises designed to help actors share their private selves with an audience. She does not use such exercises very much in practice, but she feels that the experience of such training in a class was very valuable to her. It helped her get over the fear of sharing very personal things with others. She is no longer embarrassed by her own emotions: '...if you want to be creative as an actor, you have to be prepared to make a fool of yourself.'[68] The Welsh actor Michael Sheen has stressed how frightening overcoming inhibitions can be. While being as exploratory as possible, '...you have to be prepared to look like a complete idiot in front of your fellow actors.'[69] Sheen also believes that people obsessed with the preservation of a particular self, or personality – in other words, those who, unlike actors, cannot face the investigation of their true selves – end up by destroying themselves. For him, personality is not an expression of the true self, but is rather a defence against it. We need this conflict to survive in the world, but it can also destroy us.[70]

The fear of embarrassment is what prevents many people from being able to act in public; it is wrong, however, to assume that actors do not suffer similar embarrassment: they have simply learned how to utilise it, make it work for them, or, if they find it difficult to overcome, they have devised ways of escaping from it – most commonly by being someone else. The actor Roger Rees has explained how scared he has always been of performing in public. He finds even walking about difficult. When he has a long speech he does it as quickly as he can, to get it over with. It is his way of dealing with fear. A little later he adds: 'It's me fighting against myself, and I think that's what acting is about.'[71] The extremes to which an actor must go to overcome embarrassment have been stressed by the stage, television and film actress Eileen Atkins. For her, you should not be an actor unless you are willing to reveal everything that is inside you: 'I've been on stage stark naked covered with shit (in *Mary Barnes*), so I'm not somebody who's holding back...'[72]

Simon Callow has commented that the first time he felt he was truly acting was when he was able to forget about himself, how well he was performing, what others thought of him, etc. For the first time since he had joined the Drama Centre he felt he was not performing, and he was beginning to understand what playing a character meant. It meant giving in to another way of thinking: 'I was *being in another way.*' He feels that any talent for acting that he might possess involves the ability to cast aside his own self-consciousness. In doing this he discovers a new liberating energy.[73]

It would thus seem that actors, while, like the rest of us, being unable to bear many unpalatable aspects of their own selves, are nevertheless willing to let down their defence shields, contemplate those aspects, and then either utilise them in some way or devise ways of escaping from them into other personalities. Eileen Atkins has said that she does not understand actors who just want to become famous and earn a lot of money. For her, the real joy of acting is in persuading people that you are someone else, entering into the being of someone else entirely. She quotes a comment by Alec Guinness, which pleased her, on one of her performances: 'Eileen, you were marvellous. I could not see *you* at all.'[74] Nigel Hawthorne had always felt acting to be a way of escaping from painful shyness into being someone else; as a child he had felt himself to be rather plain and was very self-conscious. It was a great relief when he found that he could hide himself behind all kinds of strange characters.[75] Judi Dench's view is similar; she believes that you have to be a certain kind of personality to want to act, and that most actors are quite shy people: 'So I put my energies into being another kind of person, entirely different, and trying to understand another person's life. I'm happier doing that.'[76] But actors vary in the ways they perceive the process of acting a role. Simon Callow used to believe when he was younger that it was possible to become someone completely different. But, since then, he has changed his mind, believing it is neither possible nor desirable for him to become someone else entirely. He would not prescribe the same attitude for other actors, however, because he feels that each actor must follow his or her own compulsions. Acting means very much working together with the audience: 'I now very much see my work as an actor as finding a meeting point between me and the person envisaged by the audience...'[77]

However actors may describe their state of mind during the process of becoming another person, it is clear that some kind of psychological instability, cultivated or otherwise, is necessary. Fiona Shaw has described it as a 'binary state'. On the one hand acting consists simply in walking about and talking, but it is more than that: the actor has to see 'the possibility or significance of those moments...' And thus, for her, acting is clearly an intuitive matter, which is why she believes that actors are born and not made. The basic ability to act must be there to start with: 'They have to have a fundamental ability to be in a binary state, in permanent dialogue with their own imaginations...'[78]

For Anna Deavere Smith, actors never actually become the person they seek to be. They inevitably remain in that intermediate 'binary state'. She defines acting first in terms of what it is *not*: it is not *being*. In this, she goes against the essence of the training she received, which taught her to find the character within herself and that acting was a form of existing, but on a stage. However, she gradually realised that this led to what she describes as 'a spiritual dead end'. Her aim as an actress is to establish a connection between herself and the character: 'Acting is really about building a bridge between the self and the other.' She quotes the concept, coined by the critic Richard Schechner, of the 'not not'. This is the point you reach, as you try to be the character, where you are not yet the character but you are also no longer yourself. This is a positive state, and for her it is the most that an actor can hope to achieve, because she believes that she can never really *be* another person. The actor creates a fiction, but that fiction can reveal great truth.[79]

All actors are agreed on the 'high' they feel when they

successfully perform as another person, however they explain the process to themselves psychologically. Ian Richardson recalled the first experience he had of having a powerful effect on an audience: 'It's an experience I've had only a few times in my professional life, but it can happen. It's a moment of magic...'[80] It is the 'high' of becoming a much more exciting person. In the words of Elaine Stritch: 'Acting is a game of pretending: you're not you, you are someone else; someone far more interesting, exciting and dramatic.'[81] Talking of herself when younger Fiona Shaw has said: 'I suppose I was full of the need to show off. If you took away the moral unattractiveness of the desire to show off, I would say it was a need to experience life at a heightened frequency...'[82] And Simon Callow describes the actor giving a good performance as 'the human being functioning at its highest level'. This does not imply that it is also functioning at its deepest level, but it is exercising itself in an extremely demanding way, practising what he calls 'callisthenics of the psyche'. You feel energy pumping through your whole body: 'Life can sometimes seem a sad second.'[83]

REALISM AND TRUTH

Actors frequently speak of the goal of their acting as being the attainment of truth, though what this truth consists of proves difficult to define. It most often seems to imply an ideal of insight into the essence of the character being played and an appropriateness in the performance. Jane Lapotaire, who has been a member of the Royal Shakespeare Company and also a founder member of the Young Vic Theatre, has said: 'Good acting is about being truthful, whether you're truthful to a camera that's three feet away from you, or whether you're truthful to an auditorium that holds two thousand people...'[84] It is interesting that this truthfulness is conceived as being directed towards the audience. Thus, while all may be pretence, one must not, paradoxically, deceive. Talking of acting for film, Ian Richardson has said: 'It is important to make friends with the camera, and still more with the camera operator. And you *must* be truthful, and let your soul show through your eyes.'[85] For Anthony Sher, all good acting is Method acting in that it's utterly truthful.[86] For Miriam Margolyes, too, there is little difference between stage and film acting with regard to the truthfulness of a performance. Whether the focus is entirely on her or not, she still has to be as real: 'I still have to be [...] as truthful as possible, whether the spectator is close or not, present or not...'[87] And Linda Marlowe concurs that actors have to find truth and reality whatever the medium they are performing in.[88]

Seeking for truth is clearly associated in many actors' minds with the concept of Method acting, and with the names of specific gurus in America, Lee Strasberg and Uta Hagen. For Ruth Posner, Method acting meant that three things had to be emphasised: observation, accuracy and the pursuit of truth.[89] Liev Schreiber interpreted the Method as Lee Strasberg's way of helping actors find emotional truth and source memories with which they could inform the text.[90]

Reality and truth would seem to be two sides of the same coin for an actor: if you can somehow be truthful, to yourself, to the character, to the audience, then that lends reality to the character; to be truthful is to make real. Gwen

Ffrangcon-Davies has said that she has always tried to find the essential reality of whatever she was speaking, making it clear without too much stress. She asked herself always only three questions: 'Is it real? Is it true? Do I believe it?'[91] This criterion of truth is considered to be relevant to whatever kind of acting one is required to do, whether for a classical play or a modern one. Athene Seyler has perhaps come closest to classifying what such truthfulness consists of; for her, the only really necessary thing in all acting is truth. If you think about the truth of everything you do, then everything else comes right: thinking, speaking and walking. To the question of how one actually discovers that truth, her answer is very down to earth: '…you dig about in the play you're doing and find it – the truth of a scene or the truth of a relationship.' If you then keep that truth in your mind, you are most likely to speak the words in the right way. You will grasp intuitively when to hurry, when to pause, etc. Other than that she does not believe that it is possible to lay down any rules.[92] In other words, if you truly understand what is going on in your character and in the scene, then the way of speaking and behaving will follow naturally. In period plays this means actually understanding the functions of contemporary props and items of costume and not just imitating gestures in an empty way, for in that lies meaningless stylisation. Thus, even in apparent superficialities, pertinent truth can be found. Peter Barkworth has written about something Dame Edith Evans told him: '"*You* mustn't be stylised," she said, and started talking about how to use a fan. "Those eighteenth-century ladies didn't use their fans for *style*, they *used* them."' She went on to explain that they fanned themselves if they were hot or embarrassed. They could poke someone with their fans, or slap someone with them if they were cross. Truthfulness consists in finding out how people of the time actually dealt with their various accessories, such as wigs, clothes, etc.[93]

It should be remembered, however, that being truthful and finding the reality of a character is not necessarily the same as being natural. Naturalism on the stage is also a semblance: an actor creates the illusion of being natural. Edward Petherbridge once said, 'To be natural is just another kind of artifice.'[94] John Hurt (famous for *The Elephant Man*, *10 Rillington Place*, etc) told Peter Barkworth that he was sick of naturalism: 'We are entertainers, after all... and we need a sort of heightened naturalism.'[95] Eileen Atkins tells a story about Sir Laurence Olivier, who asked her during the run of a play they were both in why she was always late on a certain entrance. She explained that she had to run up the off-stage stairs and down them again before entering. His response was, 'Darling, you're off-stage. It's magic on stage, not reality, magic.' And he solved the problem for her: she needed only run halfway up the stairs, because the audience could not see her offstage and therefore would not know she had not run all the way up. Eileen Atkins said she learned an invaluable lesson from this: that the art of acting is making people think it's reality when it isn't. She added: 'But if you do total reality on stage, mostly it doesn't work.'[96]

PREPARING A ROLE

It is generally accepted nowadays that all actors should have some training in 'technique'. It is claimed that this is what distinguishes the professional from the amateur. Professional actors have to perform night after night unfailingly, and to maintain high standards they must have stamina, be in good physical condition, have a well-trained voice, etc. Good amateur actors are also concerned about such matters but are usually involved in only very short runs. Advice on seeking such training is provided later in this book. Professionals and amateurs are, however, on a par concerning the matter of preparing a role. It is true that one can be trained to do this better, to improve the way one sets about preparing a role, but some sensitivity to human behaviour, ability to enter into the minds of others, and intellectual capability to analyse a text are prerequisites. The existence of such prerequisites is the reason for the constant recurrence of the question: is an actor born or made? The question is, of course, unanswerable. Some disposition has to be there to want to take up acting in the first place, and perhaps no one can become a good actor without such a disposition; but, as with all the arts, there has to be opportunity, encouragement, regular practice and the development of relevant intellectual attitudes for disposition to mature into competence. Assuming that professionals and amateurs have both disposition and some competence, they will both have to set about preparing roles in similar ways.

Instinct and intuition

Even many professional actors, famous ones among them, claim not to do any specific detailed preparation, but to follow their intuition most of the time. Elaine Stritch has expressed this attitude most baldly: 'I do not undertake any research; I learn my lines and listen to the director.'[97] Eileen Atkins has expanded on this process. First, she reads the part in the play and considers whether she has it within herself to play the role. Once she has decided she can do it, she does not look at the text again until the first rehearsal. The reason is that she does not like doing much work by herself. She prefers to listen to what the director says and observe what the other actors are doing: 'I don't want to have too many set ideas, because I want to be able to move.'[98]

Alan Bates has spoken of needing to 'creep up on' a character. He admits to having made the mistake several times in his life of thinking he could see a part so clearly, believing he knew exactly how he should do it, that he went for it just as he perceived it. It may be that his portrayal worked, but, in his words, 'It's not as interesting as it would have been if you'd really allowed yourself to creep up to it.'[99]

Dame Judi Dench has expressed herself vividly and clearly on the matter of following one's intuition in preparing a role. She admits that, on the first day of rehearsal, she has absolutely no idea of what she is doing: she just starts work on the role. She does not do any preparation prior to this. The only thing she needs is to be told the story of the play. Then she lets her subconscious mind take over. There are occasions when something is suggested to her by the director, but she does not do anything about it there and then. She just sleeps on it. Then the next day things somehow work out: 'I never underestimate that extraordinary side of ourselves.'[100] She does undertake a lot of research but not before rehearsals start. One metaphor vividly clarifies the process she adopts. She describes it as being like picking up a piece of a jigsaw, without knowing what the whole picture will be. At first, you just see all the jumbled-up parts. Then you start to recognise individual colours, details in other actors, and suddenly you are able to start putting bits of the puzzle together.[101]

Interestingly, the actress Janet McTeer uses the same metaphor to describe researching a role based on a real person. When she was preparing for her role in the BBC production of Nigel Nicholson's *Portrait of a Marriage* she read everything available on Vita Sackville-West and also spent many days in her house at Sissinghurst. Especially when working on a real-life character, she feels it is like putting little bits of a jigsaw together. Eventually, she has to find the one piece in the middle which corresponds to herself, with which she feels she can connect and which also makes all the individual pieces disappear as the whole picture emerges.[102] Thus, whether you follow instinct or research thoroughly, whether it is an imaginary character or one based on a real person, the jigsaw analogy would seem a good one.

Most actors would seem to agree on the need for there to be an initial instinctive feeling for a role. Jane Lapotaire has said that her instincts have to respond to what is on the page, and she has to feel empathy with the character.[103] According to Janet McTeer, being in a state of ignorance and confusion at the start is actually a good creative condition to be in. For her, it is necessary to assume that she knows nothing about the character at the beginning. It is like painting a new picture on a blank page. Starting with a sense of chaos is therefore a good thing, because it means that everything is possible. She believes that if you try to impose a particular way of working, then it will be constricting.[104] It is a 'horses for courses' approach that many actors adopt. Stephen Rea is one. He doesn't have any fixed idea or method, because he doesn't think you can. Every role must be considered differently. Sometimes intuition is the key thing: one follows it, and it works. For other roles, more research and investigation of the part are needed.[105] Sometimes, indeed, it is best for the actor's own mental balance and the success of the performance if he or she is not fully aware of how the characterisation was accomplished. Of his role as a powerful politician in the television drama *House of Cards* Ian Richardson said that he realised he needed to create an aura of power. He did not know exactly how he achieved this, and compared it with making love: even if he could have explained it, he wouldn't have done, because it would have spoiled it for him. All that he was willing to say was that he got there by digging very deeply.[106]

Study and research

With all the instinctive 'digging', however, clearly, for most actors, some degree of close study of the character, even if it is only the words on the page – and the historical background, if the play is set in period or based on real people – becomes necessary. When and how, and to what extent will vary from actor to actor.

About his preparation for the role of Diaghilev Alan Bates has said: 'I do research until I feel that there's no room for me; until I feel that I've been almost locked out of it by other people's opinions, say, about Diaghilev. In the end you've got to be him yourself, you've got to find him for you.' Thus, for Bates, there came a moment when he realised that he had to cut off. If he read too much, he ended up playing the character as conceived by someone else, rather than providing his own interpretation.[107]

An actress who has similar views about researching within measure is Brenda Fricker. She admits that she used to explore closely the motivation of the character, imagining what their past was like and what their various interests were, but finally she found that, as long as the script was well written, it was not necessary to do a large amount of research and what she describes as personalisation. For her, good writing is like poetry, very economical in its means of expression, and the danger is not lack of understanding but excessive analysing. It is possible to destroy a character by over-analysing it. This attitude arises from a modesty about the possibility of understanding human psychology: 'I haven't a clue what goes on in my own head, never mind trying to find out what goes on in somebody else's head.'[108] Nigel Hawthorne was another actor who respected the need for research but felt that there was always a point at which all research had to be put aside. When he played real-life people he certainly did the relevant research (as for his roles as Pierre Curie and CS Lewis in *Shadowlands*), but then he discarded it: 'You can't play research.' One tip he learned the hard way was, 'Play the script.'[109] Anthony Sher is also a researcher and discarder. He has said that he loves researching and does a lot for most of his roles, but he always ends up throwing a lot of it away.[110] Asked how he takes more control over a performance, especially of a Shakespearean role, Liev Schreiber replied that he studies everything as diligently as he can and then forgets it all, because in the end it does not matter. But he does admit to reading everything he can because one never knows when a particular discovery might be useful: 'It's a process I go through partly out of neurosis and partly because I care about my role.'[111]

Ian Richardson stressed that it all depends what information you are given in the text of the play. In some plays, whether the character is fictional or non-fictional, there is so little information about the character that the actor has to invent a lot of background before beginning to interpret the character's behaviour. This background is not disclosed to the audience 'but it will help the actor breathe some life into the part'. For him, there are a few parts, 'jewel-like in their construction', where everything you need is given in what they say, and he cites General Burgoyne in *The Devil's Disciple* and Sir Robert Morton in *The Winslow Boy*: '…they are known in the trade as actor-proof.'[112] The present writer, having himself played the role of Sir Robert Morton in *The Winslow Boy*, and certainly lacking Richardson's genius, has to admit that he found it necessary to imagine a specific psychological profile for Sir Robert, to account for the self-control and distance of the man. The director and actors were never informed about this profile, out of fear that it might not be approved of. It worked well for the performance, however, which was critically well received.

For Willem Dafoe, how much preparation you undertake depends on how close you feel to the character you are to play: 'For me, you do whatever it takes to give you the authority to pretend; you do whatever makes you feel you have the right to be this person.'[113]

Some actors feel the need to have an imaginary biography for all the characters they play. By her own admission, Anna Massey works in this way. In a discussion with Peter Barkworth about her performance as Miss Prism in *Blithe Spirit*, she said she felt that a major challenge was how to be eccentric, pointing out that Margaret Rutherford, famous in the role, had her own natural eccentricity, which she brought to it. The first thing she did was to work out a biography for the part, as she always does. And she does this well before the start of rehearsals. 'I like to know what my parents were like; and whether I have brothers or sisters. And I cast them. From old friends, new friends, people I've seen in the street. Then I can see them. In my mind's eye. Images. I like to know the house where I was born, the school I went to and, most definitely, where the play takes place.' Just having this biography in her mind is the important thing, and it is not used consciously in performance: 'You see, when I work out these biographies I don't know what the result will be. I don't play the result.'[114]

There is even a danger for the actor's own psychological state in pursuing research of a character too obsessively. David Suchet discovered this in his portrayal of Sigmund Freud. He regards it as a cathartic moment in his career, but it was also the most dangerous, because he felt that he became the character to a greater extent than he had ever done before.[115] Suchet researches his fictional roles as thoroughly as his non-fictional ones. For his portrayal of Hercule Poirot he read every single book by Agatha Christie.

He attempts to make his performance a blend of what he perceives the character to be and his own personality. He draws up two columns, one listing the similarities of the character to himself and the other the differences. He then completely ignores the similarities and never thinks about them again, focusing instead on the differences. Thus, somehow, the two blend together and become his interpretation.[116] Peter Barkworth has formulated very much the same idea in the form of practical advice in his book *About Acting*: 'There is no question of obliterating yourself and starting a characterisation from scratch. Mostly you use yourself, and change only what is necessary. "Accept what is the same, and alter what is different," said Fabia Drake, one of my teachers at RADA, and that's it.'[117]

There are occasions, however, when an actor finds a character to be completely at odds with his or her own personality but still has to find a way of playing the role. Janet Suzman has described the difficulties she had in realising the role of Alexandra in the film *Nicholas and Alexandra*. She felt that Alexandra was the opposite of everything she was. Alexandra was very right-wing and Lutheran, narrow-minded and not very intelligent. She found access to the character eventually through the fact that Alexandra had a haemophiliac son. She could understand, as any mother would, how obsessed Alexandra would be with her child. Through this she gained further understanding of her behaviour towards Rasputin and the Russian people in general, which was very much governed by her concern for her son.[118]

Discovering Objectives

The matter of training will be considered later, but many actors have admitted that when they encounter some difficulties in developing a role they will resort to what they learned in their training, especially to what are known as objectives, which are basically the motivations of the character in the play. Penelope Wilton has said that she has found it useful to break down her script into objectives, asking herself questions such as: Why is she there? Where should she be? How should she do things? She adds: 'Sometimes you know immediately and instinctively what to do, but if you have a problem, I think it's a very good thing to fall back on, and say "What actually am I doing in this scene?"' With maturity and experience she finds that she has to take such approaches less and less. Going back to a close study of the text is sufficient. When she encounters a problem, however, she reverts to asking herself what she is actually doing in a particular scene. Very often this means analysing the text again. She describes herself as very text-orientated, which she feels is typical of English actors, who learn to consider the text and good speaking of the text to be very important. She believes that the text is what differentiates the theatre from every other medium, which can do everything else much better. She retains the belief that theatre is in some way magical and that this magic resides in the words and the stories told.[119]

Margaret Tyzack, a highly accomplished and experienced actress, also finds the term 'objective' useful in describing how she prepares a role. She still turns to one old teacher and friend, Elizabeth Pursey, when she needs help: 'She would say, "Never do something until you feel with every fibre of your being that it is the only way you could express what you want to do."' She had noted down once, in order to remind herself, the thought that an actor must 'earn the right' to speak his or her line. She believes that one should perceive the lines as being at the end of a process. The actor must find out what the character is seeking to achieve in every scene, indeed in every line, and narrow this down until it becomes so specific 'that the lines written down are the only means of expressing it'. Another dictum she formulated for herself was 'Not how you say it but why you say it.'[120]

STANISLAVSKY AND THE METHOD

A brief survey of Stanislavsky's ideas has already been provided near the end of the historical survey of acting styles in section one. There it was also stressed that he was, for the most part, only formulating what all good actors, all good naturalistic actors at least, have always known and practised. What came to be known as the 'Method', primarily in America, was a development and modification of his views to suit the needs and different circumstances of actors in the West. The names Lee Strasberg and Michael Chekhov are especially well known as proponents of this approach. When interviewed about how they prepare and develop a role, many actors and actresses will cite Stanislavsky, Strasberg, Michael Chekhov and often one book specifically, *Respect for Acting* by Uta Hagen. The term 'Method' is often used loosely by actors and critics to refer to the whole approach to preparing a role in depth.

Comments vary from the enthusiastic to the dismissive.

Talking of his experience of being trained at the Drama Centre, Simon Callow reveals mixed views of Stanislavsky. On the positive side, he feels that starting with the basic principles of the Stanislavsky system is a very good thing for a young actor to do.[121] On the negative side, he has found Stanislavsky to be a comic, naïve person, who was very cerebral, with little respect for the text and hence prone to paraphrasing. While admitting his contribution to the theory of acting, Callow criticises his generalising from his own experience to that of all actors. Stanislavsky felt extremely self-conscious on the stage, so he assumed that all actors did. Much of his technique is therefore focused on the task of making the actor forget that they are on the stage in front of an audience. For Callow, this is not liberating but narcissistic and leads to a lack of communication with the audience. Thus, while Stanislavsky provided many valuable insights into the art of acting, his ideas should not be 'treated as a bible'.[122]

He has nevertheless inspired many would-be actors. David Suchet has talked of his early enthusiasm. He was about 16 when he started reading *An Actor Prepares* by Stanislavsky. He became fascinated by the art of entering into different thought processes and into a completely different physical existence, while at the same time 'serving a play and a playwright'. He feels that he retained from his reading of Stanislavsky his concern to change the actor's attitudes and also the realisation that he could both serve the text and have the freedom to create his own interpretation.[123]

One of the best, most down-to-earth accounts of what

Stanislavsky's system is all about has been provided by the American actress Elaine Stritch, who said, in her blunt, no-nonsense way:

> We studied Stanislavsky, who rightly said that as an actor you do not do anything without a good reason. It was quite a shock, but the son of gun was right. Stanislavsky was all about reality with a capital 'R' and motivation with a capital 'M'. There was no posing; everything, every word and every move had to be straightforward and on the level; in other words, no bullshit. What is your motivation? Why are you angry with your mother? Where do you stand on the stage to express this anger?[124]

Some actors feel, however, that more physical activities, including improvisations, can be used to gain the same results as self-conscious analysis. Conrad Nelson has said that he used to find these more interesting than using Stanislavskian methods, but admits that he now enjoys doing both. For him, Stanislavsky's approach, involving psychological analysis of the character, is just one of many possible methods available to the actor.[125] William H Macy, greatly influenced by the playwright and theorist David Mamet, argues that there is good and bad in Stanislavsky's ideas. He believes that there are two sides to Stanislavsky's theories: one concerns physical action and discovering objectives, and the other focuses on the character's emotional life. For Macy, Stanislavsky's theory of emotions does not work, for the simple reason that it is impossible to control one's emotions. If it is possible to find truth in emotions, then it is not to be found through conscious reflection, because such truth exists in the subconscious. Any technique employed by the actor must therefore involve a way of liberating emotional truth spontaneously: 'I think actors should put their attention on what they want – on the objective – and let the emotions take care of themselves.'[126]

Simon Callow has provided some perceptive comments on the work and ideas of Lee Strasberg, which help to understand the differences between American and British styles of acting as stressed by many actors (see later section on this topic). For him, Strasberg focused narrowly on the emotional aspects of Stanislavsky's theories, which led to the encouragement of actors to be closely in touch with their emotions. The result is actors who are superb at expressing extremes of emotion but little else. For Callow, Strasberg's methods are ideally suited to developing acting skills suitable for soap operas, because the performances in such drama are all about emotional exposure and endless crisis. There is no concern about the use of language, form or ideas.[127] Of Strasberg's Actors Studio Judi Dench has said that she considers it too introverted for her. It is too much concerned with the self and not with the audience. She recalls seeing something at the Studio and not being able to hear a word.[128] David Suchet has a similar view about the Method in general. His reservations about it also concern the inability of the actors who practise it to project themselves sufficiently on the stage. Then acting becomes self-indulgence: 'They cease to serve the piece, and only serve themselves.' In such circumstances actors are 'losing a generosity of spirit'.[129]

For Ian Richardson, trained at a college with a principal

who was an exponent of Stanislavsky, the Strasberg Method School is essentially a debased version of the Stanislavsky system. He felt quite strongly that the Method School and Stanislavsky are poles apart: 'Stanislavsky is never overindulgent, which the Method is. Stanislavsky is never incoherent, which the Method is. Stanislavsky is controlled and technically polished, which the Method could never be.'[130] He does not dismiss the Method entirely, however, because he believes that all sensitive actors do intuitively what the Method prescribes. Method consists of what any sensible and sensitive actor would do anyway. It errs by ignoring the technical aspects of acting, such as projection and clarity of diction. Truth is one thing, but it is a waste of time if no one can hear what you are saying.[131]

THE VOICE

The point on which all actors are agreed is that it is important to develop and maintain a good voice. Whatever else an actor must be concerned about, the voice is the most crucial to his or her art. From her voice teacher at LAMDA, Iris Warren, Janet Suzman retained one lesson above all: that an expressive voice is the only tool that an actor really needs, 'just like a musician needs a well-tempered instrument.'[132] To maintain the voice, and be able to use it in various ways at will, requires attention to many auxiliary functions which enable it to work well, and to features of language.

Breathing

In order to use the voice extensively and reliably without it letting an actor down, good breath control must be mastered. Harry Andrews admitted to learning much about how to improve his breathing and its relation to voice production from the same teacher as Janet Suzman, though in private sessions: he found that he was using what he called 'strangulated voice, not releasing from the throat'. Iris Warren made him lie on his back and do exercises to relax. He had to make special noises and not utter actual dramatic speeches. Finally, she had him sing something, to use his vocal cords fully.[133] Gabrielle Daye has expressed herself much more technically on the subject of control of the breath specifically. She was taught the rib-lateral or intercostals method, by which you take breath into the lower part of your ribs and flatten the diaphragm. She compares it to a singing exercise in which it is necessary to take as deep a breath as possible and let it out very slowly.[134] Robert Stephens is equally lucid on the technical aspects: 'You have to use diaphragmatic control. You have to lift the ribcage and keep it lifted, which means you spread all the intercostal muscles and fill yourself with as much air as you can get. Take the breath when the other person is speaking, two lines before he finishes his speech, so you are ready to carry on, bang, bang, bang. If you are running out, just lift it again.'[135]This would seem to be very much the same method which Gwen Ffrangcon-Davies learned when she was young. She was taught to breathe in her diaphragm. This gave her what she describes as a 'cushion' for her voice to rest on, which prevents it from being strained.[136] But many actors acquire good breathing more intuitively. Alec Guinness has said that he never had any vocal trouble. He just consciously took a breath where it seemed to him that he needed it, to maintain the flow of the line till the end.[137] With long speeches or fast song lyrics, of course, the breathing is crucial, and sometimes there simply is not time for deep breaths. Rex Harrison managed by using 'snatched breaths'. In this way he did not need to fill his lungs with a large amount of air before starting something.[138]

Vowels and Consonants

Articulating words clearly and audibly is very much the concern of all those actors who are not extremely self-involved devotees of the Method. This involves being able to control the sound qualities of vowels and consonants at all times. One of the simplest and, indeed, most amusing ways of improving mastery and building self-confidence in articulation is through the frequent practice of tongue-twisters of the 'Peter Piper picked a peck of pickled peppers' variety. There are now many collections of them available, both in book form and on websites. They are also frequently used in the teaching of foreign languages and can be found in EFL (English as a Foreign Language) textbooks. There is a selection of useful ones for actors in Peter Barkworth's *About Acting*.

Some actors consider the clear articulation of consonants to be the most important. Gwen Ffrangcon-Davies has said: '...and a technical thing for audibility is consonants. Vowels will take care of themselves.'[139] And Patricia Hayes has pointed out that vowels will reveal the accent of the character more clearly than the consonants, but that comprehensibility will very much depend on good articulation of the consonants. It must be possible to hear 'the t and the d and p and the b'.[140]

Projection

Another important skill related to the technical aspects of voice production is projection: the ability to make one's voice heard clearly over a considerable distance. This is not the same as having sufficient volume or loudness. In the words of Fabia Drake: 'The primary job of the actor is to be audible.'[141] Actors develop an intuition for how far they have to project their voice in any given auditorium. Rex Harrison has said: 'One's terribly conscious of getting used to hitting the back wall.' He did not have to arrange for someone to check for him if he was projecting sufficiently well: 'You sort of sense it. I generally come and have a look at it with the house lights up. Don't have to do or say anything. Just my eye tells me what the "throw" is.'[142]

Madoline Thomas has described the task of projecting well in clear, non-technical language: 'All right, take your breath, open your mouth and speak. It isn't a matter of how loud your voice is, never let anyone tell you that. It doesn't matter if you've only got a small voice as long as you say the words very, very distinctly, and remember that they're not only going to the front row.'[143] Clive Barker, on the other hand, has attempted to describe the process in a more technical way. He defines two different modes of using the voice to gain attention: what he calls the 'scattering' and the 'gathering' impulses. We use both of them commonly in everyday life: 'In physical terms this is the difference between an outward or inward flow of movement. In vocal terms an absurdly simple example lies in the difference between calling in the cat and shooing away birds. In the former the gathering impulses predominate, in the latter the scattering.' In relation to acting, specifically, he defines the process in terms which suggest that the concept of projection is wrongly conceived: 'Every actor knows that, in playing in large auditoria, the clearest audibility is never achieved by trying to push or project the voice to reach the furthest seat, but by pulling or drawing the back of the auditorium to you. A gathered impulse has a clearer focus than a scattered one, which soon dissipates its clarity in space.'[144]

STRESS AND PARTS OF SPEECH

One technique that all actors have to learn, either intuitively or through instruction, is how to stress words for the maximum impact. This usually involves sacrificing what is not crucial. Try to bring out the nuance and nicety of every single phrase and you lose the sense of the whole. Sir Michael Redgrave once noted, after seeing a production of a Shakespeare play: 'The actors – or at least some of them – seemed so intent on thinking every line and almost every phrase and occasionally even single words, that one sometimes lost the total sense of what they were saying. We actors frequently under-estimate the quickness of an audience's mind.'[145] Redgrave also reminds us that this is an age-old truth about acting. The Roman writer Cicero recognised it: 'Cicero, describing the delivery of the actor

Roscius, tells us how in certain speeches the actor would carefully prepare his big effects by deliberately sacrificing previous effects.'[146]

In the course of experience, many actors become aware of which parts of speech need to be stressed the most in order to avoid the two extremes of careful enunciation of every single word and mindless gabbling. Alec Guinness has told an interesting story about one actress who helped him a lot when he was young and who was greatly admired for her powerful stage presence and sonorous voice: Martita Hunt. She offered to give him some private lessons:

> Very rarely do I rely on any rule of thumb but Martita gave me one, at that time, which has stood me in good stead. Unless there is reason to the contrary, she taught me that, in speaking, the verb, which is the driving force of a sentence, should have first importance, then the noun, and that the adjectives and adverbs would take care of themselves and that personal pronouns should never be emphasised except in special circumstances.[147]

It is interesting to note how Clive Barker reinforces this view in more theoretical terms. He writes of a phenomenon called 'kinaesthetic feedback': the effects that words have on the body, subconsciously, because of their meanings, functions and associations. With this concept in mind he lists a hierarchy of words: 'The hierarchy of words I arrange in an order of importance. The order is established by the associated effect they have in the body through the kinaesthetic feedback. "And", for instance, produces next to no effect in me, because it is a conjunction which simply links thoughts, ideas and images.' Top of the list are verbs: 'Verbs come at the top of the list because they refer to activities, and are therefore closely associated with the process of action in the body. I look carefully at the use of verbs, their tenses and forms.' He clarifies: 'The verbs are usually the most important parts of a speech because they reveal and define the *action* that the dramatist has embodied in it, what is happening and in what terms.' Next come nouns: '*Nouns* hold the second place in the hierarchy of words since they embody images that the body responds to, or reacts to, kinaesthetically.' Finally come adjectives, adverbs and pronouns:

> *Adjectives* and *adverbs* define the precise nature of nouns and verbs. When distinctions have to be made they often take a stronger stress. The same is true of pronouns and personal pronouns. It is a minor problem that actors sometimes give adjectives and adverbs a higher place in the sentence because they indicate degree... actors, given an adjective or adverb of degree in a sentence, will at times hit it hard at the expense of the noun or verb it qualifies, and the precise sense of the line is generalised, or lost.[148]

Perhaps the last word on the matter of stress can be left with Alec Guinness:

> My chief bugbear in life generally at the moment is false emphasis. I catch a train from Waterloo and I hear an asinine girl's voice saying 'The three-EIGHTeen FOR Bournemouth WILL leave from platform...' and you're in

doubt immediately. Did she think it wasn't going to leave and they changed the platform? It seems so simple to leave things alone and let the verb tell the story, which is what it does.'[149]

RESPECTING PUNCTUATION

An important aid to getting the pace and stress right in speaking the words of a playwright is something which is there, visibly, in the text, and invisibly, notionally, when we speak in ordinary conversation: punctuation. In writing, punctuation is a way of distinguishing statements or parts of statements from each other and/or of showing how they are related to each other. When we read, either in silence or aloud to others, punctuation enables clarification of meaning and structure.

In his book *Acting Shakespeare* Sir John Gielgud writes of the importance of punctuation in Shakespeare's works, but what he writes has wider implications for plays in general. Remembering the time when he was a young actor he writes:

It seemed to me that if you were not quite sure of a very difficult speech in Shakespeare, and you studied the punctuation and got it right, the sense would in some way emerge... I tried to trust to the sweep of every speech, and to mark the commas and full stops and semi-colons, and if I observed these correctly, as a bad swimmer begins to trust the water, the text seemed to hold me up.[150]

Another actor who has found it very useful to respect the punctuation is Harry Andrews. Again, of reading verse, he has said: 'I use the punctuation as it is written – use a full stop when it's there, or a dash, or whatever.'[151]

Clive Barker has also stressed the value of making oneself aware of the punctuation. After a discussion of appropriate speed of delivery and the need sometimes to slow down the whole process, he points out that, once we have slowed a speech down, there are various ways in which the line can be broken up into its separate parts. One of these ways is to make use of the punctuation provided by the dramatist, or editor, in the text: 'By speaking the punctuation in the line, one gives full weight to the pauses which break up the line. It is easy to assign time values to commas, full stops, semicolons, etc.' He admits that texts are mostly set out according to strict grammatical principles and do not reflect the way we speak, '...but it helps the actor to make decisions about what pauses, and length of pause, he wants to make in a speech. And it leads him to an analytical examination of the structure of the text, so as to discover its precise meanings and intentions.' Admittedly, it is not usually possible to undertake this exercise for an entire role in a play, but is a useful approach to adopt for difficult passages, and if one does it often enough it becomes a reflex action: 'The brain is programmed to work this way on all texts it meets, and will often do so naturally with very little training.'[152]

There are also some interesting reflections on the emotional values and effects of punctuation in Stanislavsky's book *Building a Character*.

Punctuation signs require special vocal intonations... Without these intonations they do not fulfil their functions... In each of these intonations there is a certain effect; the exclamation sign for sympathy, approval or protest; a colon demands attentive consideration for what follows, and so on. There is great expressiveness in all these... Take the comma... It possesses a miraculous quality. Its curve... causes listeners to wait patiently for the end of the unfinished sentence.[153]

LEARNING THE LINES

There are two crucial questions relating to the problem of learning the lines for a part: when and how. The answers reveal that the processes of learning the lines and understanding the character are interdependent. The question of when you should learn the lines resolves itself into two options: should you learn the lines before rehearsing or while rehearsing? Both actors and directors differ in their opinions, with strong arguments on both sides.

The main problem about learning a role in advance of rehearsals is that the actor easily becomes set in certain ways of saying and interpreting the text. Alan Bates has warned against learning one's script at this stage, unless you only have a few days before the first performance. If you know it all already, it is fatal, because you are stuck with it in the way you learned it. It is far better to make sure that you have enough rehearsal time and to learn it as you go.[154]

Eileen Atkins has similar views, granting also that it is sometimes necessary to master your lines in advance. But she stresses that the problem, if you do learn the lines beforehand, is that you are very much 'set in railway lines'. In learning them, you have already drawn some conclusions, and it is more difficult to change things once they are fixed in your mind. She admits, however, that similar problems can arise if you learn while rehearsing, because then, working with others, you start to fix your ideas, which you will eventually have to change in any case.[155] This, according to Eileen Atkins, was an argument put to her by Peter O'Toole, who learns every part before rehearsing.

Others, too, have been adamant about learning in advance. When asked once what it was like being directed by Noël Coward, Robert Stephens replied that Coward had insisted that the actors knew every line at the first rehearsal. When Stephens asked why he insisted on this, Coward replied: 'Because learning lines is very easy. Acting is very difficult. So get rid of the book. My plays are written in short lines. It's not like playing Coriolanus where you have to pick your way through.'[156]

The American actor William H Macy, an admirer of David Mamet's approach to acting, has expressed one of the most extreme views on why and how one should learn lines in advance:

You cannot act when you are memorising the lines. If you try to act whilst memorising lines, you inculcate line readings into yourself, so it is better to learn line readings by rote in monotone. Treat them as though they are gibberish, ascribe no meaning to them and memorise them as a technical exercise. You have got to be able to say them loud, fast, forwards and backwards. Never act them until you get on stage and you are looking at another person.[157]

Having already mentioned the dangers of learning lines in advance, Eileen Atkins also stresses that you do need to be able to use the words flexibly, in a way reminiscent of Macy's views, to release your mind to be creative: she believes that you learn from repetition. When you know everything inside out, you can free your mind and your feelings.[158]

There are also actors who like to do a bit of both, learning much of it before and the rest while rehearsing. Nigel Hawthorne was one: 'I do learn my scripts before I rehearse, and I know them quite well – but if I work on them too much, I can spoil it and lose the spontaneity.'[159]

Now the whole question of when to learn lines begins to merge with that of how to learn them. Peter Barkworth is at the opposite pole to Macy and clearly despises mindless rote learning. For him, learning lines also involves understanding them. If an actor has learned the lines before rehearsals, then he or she will have inevitably worked on their meaning and implications: 'Indeed, you will have learned them *by* working on their meaning, by reading them over and over again, until the words have gradually and unforcedly sunk into your subconscious.[160]

Learning through understanding is also a principle advocated by Fabia Drake. Talking of mastering a role in Shakespeare she has said: 'When I was working on Rosalind, I read it always aloud. It's a very long part – a third of the whole play, but I never had to learn it. I read it and read it because I wanted to absorb her.' Another aid to memorising a part which she recommends is writing it out from memory: 'I write out every part; I don't copy it. I write it from memory and then I go back, and if I've made a mistake, I write it again. I don't copy it because that doesn't put it in your brain.'[161] Simon Callow agrees that you should not, indeed *cannot*, learn words as such but must master the thought processes of the character:

> It is, in my experience, impossible to learn *words*: you learn the thought patterns of the character, of which the words are the inevitable expression. If you learn the *words*, you lay down rail tracks which you must follow, and any sense of the thoughts and impulses which gave rise to the words is very hard won. The only way for me to learn, at any rate, having nothing remotely resembling a photographic memory, is to ask of each fresh line, how did this line give rise to that?, and try to reconstruct the mental journey.[162]

Finally, it is worth passing on a tip Eileen Atkins learned from other actors, which was to do her lines while doing menial tasks such as cooking. It's a very useful thing to do, and so often, when I'm cooking, I go through lines. When her husband asks her something, she thus often answers completely in the character she is playing.[163]

REHEARSALS

Reams could be – and indeed have been – written about ways to conduct and participate in rehearsals. How they are conducted will depend on a myriad of factors: the nature of the play, the beliefs of the director, the time and facilities available, etc. Above all, it is important to approach rehearsals in the right spirit and with suitable expectations: expect to feel insecure, to try things and reject them over and over again, to make mistakes, to have problems with some fellow actors. But expect also that there will be moments of fun, discovery, learning from others, feeling part of a shared, organically developing, interdependent whole. What is undertaken in rehearsals is part of a continuum, an apparently never-ending process, which starts in effect from the moment an actor first reads the play and only seems to stop with the advent of the first night; and, if one has been rehearsing well, all those processes of character development and interaction with other characters continue and mature during performance. Rehearsing is a process of hesitant maturation, which cannot be hurried: one should not expect too much too soon. Janet Suzman has said that rehearsals are not for getting it right straightaway. Their purpose is to get things wrong and then find other, better ways of doing things, ways which serve both the play and the character better. She believes that actors should be constantly curious at rehearsals, asking themselves why they did something well or badly. 'Badly' means, for her, that she was overacting, trying to make the audience think she was doing it well. Good acting is the opposite of this and gives the impression that it is easy.[164]

Despite the variety of methods adopted in rehearsing a play, there are some basic technical matters which must be considered for all productions and which can only be settled in the course of rehearsing, one way or the other. Primarily these concern where the actors should position themselves on the stage and when and how they should move. This is referred to commonly as 'plotting' or 'blocking' the play.

Blocking and making moves

Traditionally, blocking was considered necessary for all performances; latterly, though, in the course of the twentieth century, many directors and drama groups have come to prefer to allow actors' movements to evolve naturally from working on the text and ideas in the play; to let the actors discover, in fact, what are felt to be the most appropriate moves. The actress Janet McTeer supports this view vehemently. She has never liked blocking and believes that, if the move is right, it will somehow happen in the course of rehearsals. She prefers a situation in which actors just come onto a stage and do the play. Nine times out of ten things go wrong, but then, on one occasion in ten, it all works well, so that you keep that way of doing it.[165]

In certain circumstances, however, some degree of blocking is clearly necessary: when you have to get a play on stage in a short time, as in repertory; when there are complex mass scenes for which some kind of choreography is needed; and with an inexperienced amateur group that includes some actors trying out their first tentative steps on the boards. Linda Marlowe has described well the pressures of working in a repertory company, in which blocking is virtually unavoidable:

The regime required extraordinary discipline: we started a play on Monday, reading it through in the morning and beginning the blocking in the afternoon; from Tuesday to Thursday we did rehearsals in the morning and learned our lines in the afternoon; and on Fridays and Saturdays we did full run-throughs of the play without the book. The process began again on Monday with a different play, and you have to remember that we were performing in the evenings. The speed of the process was terrifying but it was the best possible training for the theatre.[166]

How you arrive at the blocking is the crucial question: is it decided in advance by the director or worked out in collaboration with the actors? It may be that the director needs to set some parameters: the general area in which the action is to take place, where furniture and other fixtures are to be located, what the actors are generally doing in this space. The method with which most actors are comfortable does not involve preordained moves, but ones agreed jointly between actors and director, as part of a process of suggestion, trial and error. In the words of Peter Barkworth: 'I can't bear being given arbitrary moves arbitrarily preconceived by the director.'[167] For him, this ignores the importance of the actor's own instincts.

Many actors seem to be happiest somewhere between the two extremes of blocking everything and no blocking at all: a bit of blocking, a bit of discussion, according to the requirements of the scene, and consideration of the preferences of all involved. Eileen Atkins has said that there is no sure method and that everyone has their own. She has found that the best actors are usually straightforward in their approach. They work out the blocking and also discuss the scene, but not endlessly.[168]

All-round sensitivity

Generally, the best rehearsals occur when everyone is sensitive to everyone else's needs. Every actor needs to remember that every other actor, while being open to suggestion, is sensitive to criticism and how they are directed. Not every actor welcomes suggestions from other actors, and actors and directors need to develop a feeling for how they should handle each other. Some actors will need to mull over things for a long while with little comment from the director, who may eventually drop a few subtle hints; other actors may be clearly floundering on some occasions and the director must find the most apposite way to put in a suggestion. The actress and playwright Eve Ensler has talked of her experience working with the actress Shirley Knight. Once, she did a play of Ensler's and it took a long time for her to really find her character. Ensler learned through working with such actresses that it is a very delicate process judging when it is right to make a suggestion and when to hold back.[169] Peter Barkworth provides a firm warning on insensitivity in actors to other members of the cast – 'Take care to acknowledge that they have as many insecurities as you have' – and points out that they will probably prefer not to be watched closely, especially during early rehearsals, and will be much happier to think that you are not judging everything they do.[170]

The role of the director

There are aspects to the job of directing a play that need not concern the actor: discussing set and costume design, planning the lighting and sound, drawing up rehearsal schedules, and the like. The prime concern of the actor is the nature of the relationship with the director during rehearsals. It has already been stressed that, ideally, this should involve sensitivity to each others' needs and ways of working, and mutual respect. Some actors claim to have found this with individual directors, but relationships are often more problematic.

The limits of directing

The balance of opinion among actors seems to be that, while there are some excellent directors around, the majority are not much help. Eileen Atkins has said: 'You don't get much help from directors on the whole.'[171] For Gabrielle Daye, a director's role is rarely influential: 'If it's a good script, you follow what the author's intentions are. You might get moulded a bit by the director, though there are remarkably few good directors.'[172] The worst is obviously the extremely dictatorial kind encountered by Ian Richardson: '...standing in line with your heels together like some squaddy on a parade ground being shouted at and told your number.'[173] Penelope Wilton seems to have had better luck with directors. She has found directors to be very helpful, apart from one she did not get on with. For her, every director has had their strengths and weaknesses, but, generally, she has felt that they wanted to serve the play rather than their own interests.[174]

It seems likely that the negative views many actors have of directors may be partly due to unrealistic expectations on their part of what a director can do. The director does not have the answer to every problem which arises, but can provide an overview and the security of organisation. In

Anthony Sher's words: 'I think many actors have love-hate relationships with directors; we expect them to know everything but hate it when they tell us. The ideal director allows you creative involvement while overseeing the production.'[175]

Actors as directors

Many actors clearly feel that a director who either is also an actor or has had some acting experience has a more encouraging and supportive approach. Simon Callow, who has been both a successful actor and director, has said of his own work as a director: 'Directing is akin to teaching, and I help elucidate things for actors. My directing is pragmatic and I do not have a system as such; I simply try to dig deeper and deeper.' He sees rehearsing very much from the actor's point of view and is concerned to help them realise their role and communicate it to the audience, asking them to think about the phrasing and the melody of it. He will ask an actor to defend a certain speech against being cut, so that they become aware of its importance. He makes them consider the audience and what they would like the audience to be thinking about their character, and consequently how they can achieve such an effect.[176] Elsewhere, Callow has pointed out one of the inherent dangers in being directed by a fellow actor, though he himself is quick to stress that, being aware of it, he is very much concerned to avoid it. He feels that men, especially, often fear that he is trying to impose on them the performance that he himself would have given, had he been playing the part. But he strives to avoid this and instead enable them to make the role their own: 'I'm constantly mediating, as a director must, between them and the character and the author. So what we end up with comes from those three people, and not from any one person.'[177]

Linda Marlowe is also an actress who has directed a lot. She does not regard herself as a conceptual director with visions which she wants to impose on the production. As an actress herself she feels she can understand the technical problems actors face and help them overcome them. The advantage for her of having an actor as a director is that they know how to make actors feel comfortable in what they are doing and how to help them when they encounter a block in their development of a character. She knows that an actor needs to feel that he or she can experiment unselfconsciously without being made to feel foolish in the director's eyes.[178]

Good directing

From the actor's perspective, good directing is whatever helps them to realise their character on stage in front of an audience. Sometimes this involves the director doing nothing whatsoever for some considerable time, and encouraging the actors not to fix anything either. Alan Bates praised the director Richard Williams for his approach. Williams insisted that no actor make any firm decisions for many days. He would suddenly stop in the middle of a rehearsal and tell an actor that he or she had just made a decision, and that they weren't ready for it yet.[179] And often a director has to encourage an actor or actress not to put too much energy into the playing. Brenda Fricker has talked of working with the director Jim Sheridan: '"Less, Brenda, less. You're doing a 100% too much. Less." That was about the only note you'd get from him.'[180]

Some actors are happiest with directors who just let them get on with developing their roles and function very much as ideal members of the audience, refining the actual performance and projection of the character. Fiona Shaw has spoken of how Stephen Daldry helped her in one production: '...he'd say, "Fiona look out! Out! Out!" He was absolutely like that, and I adored him because he left the other stuff for me to do.'[181] David Suchet has also described the director as functioning as your only audience during rehearsals.[182] In a similar vein, Ayşan Çelik has said that she needs to be able 'to trust a director's eye, ear and heart'. As an actress she cannot watch herself rehearsing, and needs the director to watch her performance for her.[183]

Of another director, Deborah Warner, Fiona Shaw has said that she appreciates the way she lets her talk about things, in the belief that the inspiration has to come from the actor, with the director encouraging its growth.[184]

For Alec Guinness, a good director was clearly also someone who could engender bravery, encourage risks. Especially for young actors, he considers it important that a director point out something you had not thought of and give you the courage to dare to do something: 'It's enabling you to dare that is where they can help, as well as keeping a disciplined eye out to see that things don't get sloppy.'[185]

It is as rehearsals proceed and actors make progress in developing their characters that they need a good director to help them edit, select and refine. Wyn Jones, an actor and director, has said that a director has to work like an editor, first enabling the actor, then helping him or her to pare things down.[186] And Alec McCowan has said very much the same in other words. He likes a director who gives the actor a lot of freedom at the beginning to explore all sorts of ways of doing things. By about the fourth week of rehearsals, however, he often felt he had no sense of perspective. At this point he needed a director to help him to select what was best: 'I need a selecting man, a selecting genius, I suppose.' Of the director Michael Rudman he said that he would suddenly come to him at the last minute and say, '"You do not need that pause, you don't need to strive so hard for that effect, you don't need to make that point so clearly, trust this, trust the other." He was marvellously selective. And very sensitive.'[187]

Games and improvisations

Actors and directors differ greatly on the extent to which they like to use games, warm-up activities and the like, or to use improvisation to understand various aspects of a play. There are many books on these topics and collections of stimulating activities, some of which are recommended in the Resources section. In general, however, although they can serve a useful purpose in building relationships between cast members, in a busy schedule they can be considered a luxury unless they aid in exploring the relationships between characters in the play too. Some professional actors are quite dismissive of warm-up games as such. Eileen Atkins would do them, so as to be part of the team, but thought them rubbish: 'The same thing would have been done getting there a quarter of an hour before rehearsal, and all having coffee together.'[188]

Improvisations can be very useful and, indeed, sometimes necessary, according to the needs of the text. The present writer directed a production of Peter Weiss's complex play set in a lunatic asylum, known generally as *The Marat/Sade*. The play requires a large group of mentally deranged patients, to be present on stage throughout, at time participating in the main action, but also often going about their own concerns. As no individual characterisations are provided in the text it was necessary for each actor playing a patient to spend some time deciding what particular form of derangement they had, what their case history was, and what had caused the onset of their condition. They then had to interact imaginatively with each other in accordance with their mental condition. All this had to be worked on before integrating their performances into the rest of the play.

THE AUDIENCE

The relationship between the actor and the audience is one of the most magical, mercurial and electrifying aspects of the experience of acting. The audience is distantly intimate and masterfully submissive. It is no wonder that paradoxes abound in attempts to analyse the relationship. Actors often contradict each other in their views on the topic, but one comes to see that the contradictions can be reconciled.

Thus, on the one hand, Brenda Fricker can talk of relishing the control which an actor can exert over an audience. After working in film for a while she rediscovered the joys of playing to a live audience and how you can manipulate it: one evening she had a rowdy audience and was anxious how she could control them for a beautiful, eight-minute-long love speech that she had to deliver. Somehow she managed to do it: 'I don't know how I did it, but I got them to shut up. That was a great feeling.'[189]

On the other hand, there are experiences like that of Miranda Richardson, who came off stage distraught one night feeling she had performed especially badly, only to be greeted by a fellow actor who told her she had been exceptionally good. This made her feel that she really knew nothing about acting. She realised that you cannot control an audience completely, you cannot manipulate the connections the audience is making and their emotional responses.[190]

Then there is the experience of Simon Callow, who believes that the audience makes the actor's performance possible: it is an enabling presence.[191] Yet the actor also enables the audience. He points out elsewhere that, in rehearsals, he feels that things just disappear into thin air. The presence of an audience provides a greater formality and gives the actor more control. An actor can take the audience into the heart of an experience, enabling them to have an experience and reflect on it at the same time.[192]

In return, the audience helps the actor to gain further insight into his or her performance, into the character, into the play. Miriam Margolyes is clearly very fond of her audiences: 'I refer to audiences affectionately as "my lovely blobs" and audiences certainly show you things about a moment, a scene or a character that you might have missed; they may laugh unexpectedly, or fail to laugh, or react with silent intensity, and their responses can be very enlightening.'[193]

The audience is therefore not just a passive presence but actively participates in the play, and that involvement can so exhilarate an actor that his or her performance can thereby achieve greatness. Explaining what draws her to the theatre, Linda Marlowe has said: 'It's live and the audience almost becomes the other characters for me. They may not realise how they help you to soar and shine.'[194]

But there are, of course, audiences and audiences, and it is not always possible to build up a good creative relationship with every audience. Some audiences have expectations which they are not prepared to allow to be changed, or even partially modified. This, for Michael Sheen, has been his experience of acting on Broadway or in the West End in London, where you are working for a management whose primary concern is financial success. Most of the audience is transient and made up of tourists. The actor may wish to present to the audience something which has come to be very meaningful to him or her, but much of the time the audience may just not feel the same way about it. The mass audience in mainstream theatre are not as interested in extremes or anything that is distressing or confrontational. The result is often that a performance loses all its life. That happens when the audience does not understand what the actors are trying to do, and the actor cannot give as much as he or she wishes. In such circumstances, the performance dies.[195] Peter Barkworth has a useful tip for actors who feel suddenly one night that they have a hostile audience which is just withholding all sympathy and consequently causing the actor to lose confidence: 'What I have noticed is that, when confidence goes, attack goes too. And speed. So a good way to get the audience back on your side is to go a little louder and a little faster.'[196]

Finally, for all the paradoxes inherent in the relationship between actor and audience, both share a common goal: to connect and relate. In the words of Anna Deavere Smith: 'The actor does not produce the connection alone, the audience has to push forward also; the two have to meet in the middle.'[197]

COMIC ACTING

It is arguable that the most intimate relationship between actor and audience occurs during the performance of a comedy; certainly the relationship is most audibly reflected on such occasions, through laughter. It is intimate, yet, as in most dramatic performances, also distant. The relationship between audience and actor in a comedy is also different to that between audience and comedian in a stand-up performance. The comedian recognises the presence of the audience and, indeed, speaks directly to it; for an actor to show awareness of the presence of the audience in comedy would destroy the illusion (there are, of course, notable exceptions, as with Frankie Howerd in *Up Pompeii*). In fact, in stage comedies, evoking laughter successfully depends on pretending that the audience is not there. The renowned comic actor Rex Harrison has stressed that, when playing comedy in the theatre, it is important to appear not even to be aware that the audience is there: 'The moment they start to be there, you may be in trouble.'[198]

Tragedy and comedy

Actors who have played in both tragedies and comedies have noted both the similarities and the differences in the experience. Patricia Hayes has stressed the similarities. When asked whether she approaches comedy differently to tragedy, she replied that she thought there was 'a little bit of comedy in all tragedy, and there's a little bit of tragedy in all comedy'. If she had had the chance to play Lady Macbeth, she felt sure she could have found some comic element in her, believing that no person who is truly human does not also have a funny side.[199] Athene Seyler made some perceptive remarks on how a tragic performance is more introverted while a comic performance is extroverted; you are, in a sense, showing something funny to the audience: 'Tragic acting is yourself enduring something. Comedy acting is telling somebody else about it.'[200] Athene Seyler also wrote a book, *The Craft of Comedy*, recognised by many actors as the best thing to have been written about comic acting.

Audience moods

Knowing something of the various moods an audience can be in, and the different kinds of laughter it is possible to evoke, can be crucial to success in comedy. Wyn Jones has mentioned that this is one of the useful lessons you can gain from playing the same part in a comedy for six months on tour. He noted that people in different towns laughed at different times and in different ways. He also noticed that audiences laughed differently according to whether it was an actor they knew and liked or not. It is essentially the difference between laughing at a joke *per se* and laughing with the person who is telling it. You often laugh more willingly if it is an actor or actress you like and respond to readily.[201]

The mood of an audience is also completely unpredictable. Some nights they will laugh at everything and on others a good laugh has to be wrenched out of them. How much an audience is willing and inclined to laugh depends on many factors: their expectations, and even the day of the week (for example, a Friday-night audience is usually a little weary; on Saturday they are out for a good time, but often very demanding). Things that seemed hilarious during rehearsal may just not strike an audience seeing the play for the first time in quite the same way. Also, an audience can reveal comic elements in a play which the actors had not perceived. They can see the whole picture; individual actors cannot. General advice must therefore be to play it straight and let the laughs take care of themselves. If you have worked on the characterisation and the interactions well, the laughter will arise where suitable.

Losing and regaining laughs

Sometimes an actor discovers that he or she is getting a good laugh on a line, but is not sure how. Just as mysteriously, the laugh is lost again after a while. Many famous actors have had this experience, and some have discovered ways of recapturing lost laughs, though there is no sure-fire method. Wyn Jones discovered that it helped to put that little bit more energy into one's performance. When it happened on one occasion, he reports: 'I just said to myself that old cliché, come on, be "in it" a bit more; and just saying that made some lost laughs come back.'[202] Anna Massey has explained how she recovered a lost laugh in a production of *The Importance of Being Earnest* by thinking through again, very carefully, the whole sequence in the play: '...and I suddenly remembered what I'd done at the first preview. The line was "I think, dear Doctor, I will have a stroll with you. I find I have a headache after all." This after I've just denied having a headache. And I remembered I used to do it with such joy, almost a little skip, and that's funny.'[203] She had lost the laugh by forgetting to do this little skip of joy and doing it sadly as though she really did have a headache.

Dame Edith Evans revealed a profound understanding of the process of losing and regaining laughs to Alec Guinness. On the first night of a play he received riotous laughter from the audience on an exit line, but on subsequent nights the laugh eluded him. He was at a loss to explain it. Dame Edith reminded him that he had not understood how he got it in the first place and told him not to worry: it would take him about a week but, when he had found it again in a week's time, it would be there forever. He wondered how she could be so certain of this, and she replied that if he strived for a laugh it would not come. But as he had a natural comic gift, the laugh would eventually emerge again. Then he should remember what he was feeling at the time and reproduce that in the future.[204] Sure enough, he regained his laugh one week later.

The role of technique

Although these examples seem to indicate that comic acting is very much a matter of intuition, some mastery of technique does facilitate the process. Prunella Scales has noticed this. She believes that you need to have a natural sense of what is funny, but you can help these natural gifts with a sense of rhythm and by using different dynamics. Delivering lines at a different speed or volume can be sufficient. She explains that, by rhythm, she is thinking primarily of how one uses phrasing and stress. She feels she has learned that there is basically only one main stress in all sentences, and that this is true of all kinds of speech, of colloquial speech, of mannered speech, and of the speech needed for situation comedy. What she describes as 'rationing the stresses' has a far from dull effect: 'It's the reverse of dull: it makes speech rapid, shifting and varied, and is very good for comedy.' She cites famous comedians such as Ronnie Barker, John Cleese and Richard Briers, who have a facility with rapid speech, and a feeling for when to use stress and when not.[205]

Peter Barkworth has enumerated various points to bear in mind when doing comedy. Some involve a degree of technique, but others can be considered suitable attitudes of mind. Though it is generally regarded as necessary for all acting, it is absolutely crucial in comedy to speak clearly and not fade down at the ends of sentences. Laughs depend on good comprehension. For Barkworth, as for Prunella Scales, maintaining the overall rhythm is important: 'Keep the rhythm of the lines. Keep the flow of the feed-lines and the laugh-lines right through to the very last word. Remember that when you have a laugh-line you are not only inviting the audience to laugh but you are inviting them to laugh at a particular moment...'[206] Barkworth is a mine of wise observations on the art of comedy: 'Don't try to be funny but know what it is that's funny about the funny bits'; '...know the value of slack turns of the head during a laugh-line. I don't know why they work but they seem to, as do small involuntary movements...'; 'What most people mean by "timing" is using a beat-pause between the feed-line and the laugh-line, but... it can often be just as funny to come in on cue'; '...remember that while the audience is laughing you are pausing – the laughter does not *belong* to the stage – and the pause must be filled'; '...come in with the next line as the laughter is dying. Do not wait for it to finish.'[207] This latter technique helps maintain the theatrical illusion. Waiting for the laughter to finish signals that the actor is aware of the audience's presence. Inexperienced comic actors also often tend to try to talk through the laughter, but when an audience is laughing it is also deaf, and cannot hear what you are saying. Crucial remarks may therefore be lost. Barkworth has also stressed that the exaggeration of emotion is effective in comedy: '...so that worry becomes frenzied anxiety, smugness becomes unbearable complacency and distaste becomes anguished indignation.'[208]

Noel Coward provided some useful advice on the need to ration the amusement you provide an audience with in the course of an evening's performance. Robert Stephens, who was directed by Coward, reports Coward's use of a vivid metaphor: 'He said that, in playing comedy, what you have to do is hold the audience like a thoroughbred horse and not let them run away with you. In the first act, keep a tight rein on them and cut through every laugh. Second act, let them go a bit but not too much. Third act, let them go. He said the interesting thing about laughter is that too much can tire them out, so don't let them get tired in the first act, because you have to hit a target. The target is the final curtain.'[209] Dame Edith Evans made a similar point: 'When you're in a comedy, don't try for too many laughs in your first scene. The audience will tire of you, and be disappointed if you don't get funnier as the play goes on.'[210]

Finally, however, technique must be kept in its place, as an aid. Striving for a laugh is a sure way to lose it. In praise of the actress Penelope Keith, Peter Barkworth comments: 'She never strains for comic effect. Truth comes first.'[211]

ACTING FOR FILMS AND TV

Many actors will talk about acting for film and television by comparing it to acting on the stage. While both techniques share many features, there are important differences, and actors who have worked predominantly in one particular medium often find it difficult to adapt to the other. While many are at home in both, some prefer one to the other. There are few distinctions between acting for film and television from the actor's point of view, though the two media involve different technical conditions. When actors speak of the experience of film, therefore, or when film and television are mentioned independently of each other, their comments can generally be taken as applying to both. One fact to bear in mind is that, due to the difference in screen size, films made especially for television tend to include more close-ups than those made for the big screen – though, with the development of large mural video screens, the differences are becoming minimal.

A different process

Many actors who come to film or television from the stage are thrown by the chaos and confusion of it all. In the theatre, the actor can develop a sense of their role in the whole play and of the unity and cohesion of the production. A film is shot in jumbled chunks, one cannot easily pursue a line of development in a character, and relationships to other characters are often unclear. This is why, despite her film successes, Dame Judi Dench was still able to say in the late 1990s that she doesn't like the process. She really needs to rehearse in order to know what she's doing. She does not like having little or no time to create a character and understand things. She also dislikes the fact that a scene has to be done several times, and that the final version is often chosen not because it is the best, but because the light, focus or some other technical aspect is right.[212]

And, because everything is shot out of sequence in a film, actors have to contrive ways to maintain a sense of the whole. For his television drama series *House of Cards* Ian Richardson employed a trick he admitted learning from Alec Guinness when they were working together on the TV adaptation of John Le Carré's *Tinker, Tailor, Soldier, Spy*. Of Guinness, Richardson has said that he learns the whole script, because it's the only way to place each scene, shot out of sequence, 'in its position on the graph of your own performance.'[213]

Another thing which actors miss when working in films is the buzz of performing to a live audience. For Brenda Fricker, this is the essential difference: 'Technically, the audience is a member of the cast, which you don't have in filming. The connection there is lovely.'[214] Elaine Stritch claims that she finds no difficulty in moving from live performance to acting in film: 'Maybe I am oversimplifying, but acting for film is just getting out in front of a camera instead of a theatre audience.' However, this may be because she has developed the trick of imagining for herself an audience: 'When I do a film, I pretend that all the camera operators, the director, everybody in make-up and wardrobe, the caterers, the producer and the backers (if they unfortunately happen to be visiting the set) are my audience.'[215]

Some actors find film acting less strenuous. Janet Suzman does not mince words: '...films are physically so bloody cushy to do. Everybody looks after you, you only do short shots, so little stamina is required... Theatre's much more guerrilla warfare.'[216] Also, as David Suchet has pointed out, you can make mistakes and have off moments in film acting and they are just edited out: 'Film is more a directors' and editors' medium.'[217]

Working in short takes can also inspire an actor. It makes it possible to focus on extreme subtlety of expression. Penelope Wilton has observed that the nice thing about doing close-ups is that you can do very subtle things. After building up a scene over some time, usually less than a day, it is not necessary to do it again.'[218]

Whatever the differences between stage and screen with regard to circumstances and technique, however, an actor still has to strive for truthfulness in performance. Miriam

Margolyes has said that she still has to be as real and truthful as possible, whether the focus is on her or not.[219]

All in the mind

Anthony Sher has emphasised perhaps the most important distinction between stage acting and film and television acting. Many other actors have described the distinction with different terminology. Sher uses the terms 'stating' and 'thinking'. On the stage, the actors have to project to the back of the auditorium, which means often acting a little larger than life. But, on the screen, the way the story is told is in the hands of the director and the crew, 'so the actor can be far more complicated and enigmatic, like people are in real life. The actor can think instead of stating.'[220] Being able to put aside what is 'larger, and simpler, than life' when acting in film is very much what is meant by William H Macy when he says that, in film, theatricality is not necessary to a large extent. It requires realism and smallness.[221] Linda Marlowe also talks of 'smallness' and, although she does not say that it is in the mind, she implies it. For her, the acting style is smaller for the camera, especially in the case of close-ups. She talks of acting more internally and more with the eyes. Because of the internalisation of the performance, a film actor does not need all of the technical skills necessary for a stage actor: in film you can generally get away with less.[222] Liev Schreiber has expressed it thus: 'Film seems to lend itself to behaviour whereas theatre lends itself to action.'[223] Behaviour is sufficient because the camera can record every small detail and give the impression of looking inside the individual. In the words of

Indira Varma: 'You have to imagine that the camera can *see* your thoughts, whereas in theatre you are generally communicating your thoughts directly.'[224] This is, of course, the contrast between 'thinking' and 'stating' referred to by Sher.

The main point is summed up nicely in an anecdote told by Ruth Posner. When she was appearing in the television hospital soap opera *Casualty* she went right over the top with an hysterical reaction which would have passed muster on stage but was too 'big' for the small screen. The director took her aside and said simply: 'All you have to do is think it!'[225]

Survival tips

There are many little tips that actors have picked up here and there, often from other actors more experienced in the medium, which have helped them survive and perform successfully in the creative chaos of the film studio or of a location shoot.

When Nigel Hawthorne was working on his first leading role in a film (*The Madness of King George*, 1994), he was very worried about the whole process. His co-star, Helen Mirren, gave him two tips which he found stood him in good stead. When he was fussing and worrying about a scene she told him to let go. He should do something and basically forget about it and get on with the next shot, but she did warn him that, before doing so, it was important to be sure that he felt happy with every shot. If he was not satisfied with it, he should ask for another shot, 'because what you do will be seen for the rest of your life.'[226] The apparent contradiction between the two pieces of advice can be resolved by the notion that, in film acting, you have to learn to make decisions quickly: decide if the shot was good or not, and, if not, demand a retake; but, if it's good, forget it and move on quickly to the next.

Peter Barkworth mentions some general advice that the film director Guy Hamilton gave him: 'For filming, speak as quickly as you can and act as slowly as you can.' This enigmatic pronouncement was partly elucidated by the director in question, who explained that he never knows until he is editing how fast a scene should go. If the actor speaks quickly, he can slow it down with reaction shots, pauses, etc. But he cannot speed up a shot spoken slowly. Acting slowly probably implies slow, non-jerky movements. The same director also advised him to save up his reactions until just before speaking. Otherwise they often end up on the cutting-room floor.[227]

Samuel West has summarised the main points, or what he calls the 'golden rules', outlined by Michael Caine in a video film he made about film acting, with regard to how the actor must relate to the presence of the camera. In general, the actor must always be exactly in the right position, marked on the studio floor, and be aware that the camera picks up on the smallest error of movement and magnifies it. The actor should not blink in close-ups, and always be sure to hit his marks on the floor by pacing his walk up to them. If the camera is close and follows you rising out of a chair, then you should rise more slowly and smoothly than you would in everyday life. To avoid confusion in the viewer's mind, the actor should choose the camera-side eye of the person he or she is talking to. Don't look from eye to eye. If the actor wants to let their eyes wander, they should wander across the lens rather than away from the camera.[228]

Finally, if the advice to just 'think it' sounds too bald and general, perhaps it will be helpful to remember John Hurt's suggestion that the main ability a film actor needs is imagination and not some vague notion of being real: 'Imagining and remembering what it's like to be ill, to be frightened of illness, to be in love, to win a race, oh all these things with all their details.'[229]

AMERICAN AND BRITISH ACTING

To many, it might not seem to be very useful to distinguish between acting styles in the United States and Great Britain. When film premieres can be held simultaneously all over the world, when developed countries, and indeed developing countries, can view an actor's performance via film, satellite television or the Internet, and actors from different continents appear in the same film together, are not all acting styles tending to resemble each other? Whether this is happening or not, there are still sufficient distinctions for actors themselves to comment often on them. And a quick, superficial survey of television channels will reveal that there are indeed noticeable differences between the acting styles in, for example, drama series about murder investigations produced in America and those produced in Great Britain. These differences also hold good for the stage-acting styles of the two countries. While actors on both sides of the Atlantic are willing to admit that good acting is good acting wherever you find it, they are also aware of the general differences in emphases.

Vanity versus realism

Undoubtedly, the development of the star system and the cult of personality, especially in the American film world, have led many American actors to be more concerned about their popularity with fans than with the truthfulness of their performances. The British actress Eileen Atkins has said that she has seen good actors who have been unwilling to appear plain or ugly or portray a vicious character. They want to retain their image of niceness. For her, that is the case with American actors: they just want people to love them.[230]

Jane Lapotaire tells an anecdote which illustrates well the different priorities of British (she refers to them as English) and American actresses. She did a co-production in France for which all the English women were dressed and made up faithful to the period, with hard red mouths and formal curls. She relates that the American actresses modernised the make-up to suit their own appearance. The result was that the English looked as though they actually were from Napoleon's time, while the others seemed like characters from an American soap opera, who just happened to be wearing Empire-style dresses.[231]

Janet McTeer, reflecting on the American star system, has said that many American actors play themselves endlessly in different situations. But then, that is what it means to be a star.[232] David Suchet has never wanted to be treated like a star; he believes it would have a detrimental effect on his work. He is glad that there is a tradition of intellectual criticism of acting in England, which helps actors to have a sound perspective on their work. But the publicity which goes with stardom has only a negative effect on the actor's work.[233]

Clearly related to the prevalence of the star system, in which well-known actors are expected to play themselves over and over again, is the ease with which actors are typecast in America. Many American actors survive precisely because they are good at playing specific types. The result is that they do not get sufficient opportunities to develop themselves as actors. The British actress Janet Suzman has observed that this opportunity for development is not generally available to American actors, who are almost always asked to play the type they seem to be.[234]

Expressiveness versus technique

On the plus side, many American actors brought up in the Method school, or trained in ways resembling it, are very much concerned about their ability to express themselves in their roles. They find the emphasis on specific techniques and skills by British actors to be limiting. Margaret Tyzack tells of an American actor she knew, who was very frightened of that restriction. This was due predominantly to his not being used to the ensemble tradition.[235] However, it is clear that British actors are perceived as having the edge over American actors in general with regard to vocal skills, which are especially necessary for the gruelling nature of theatre work. Janet McTeer was surprised to discover how little voice training was undertaken in America: 'So, you get people going on stage, and they're in trouble, because they don't know how to project, or they don't know how to do it without hurting themselves.'[236]

Guts versus head

Penelope Wilton believes that many of the differences between American and British actors are due to contrasting national characters as much as to differences in training: Americans are not easily embarrassed and are more straightforward.[237] This has led to a more intuitive approach to acting in America and a more cerebral one in Great Britain. For Michael Sheen, British acting is seen as very technical, text based and vocally based, while in America acting is more emotional and perhaps more physical.[238] The negative effect of this for British acting is that many British actors have a poor sense of their physical presence and their relationships in space. Jane Lapotaire has noted that the physical side of British theatre is not a high priority. English actors tend to have a poor sense of spatial relationships and of the picture they present to the audience. She also attributes some responsibility to national character, finding that the sharp division between word-based and physical theatre in Britain is probably largely due to repression in the English character.[239]

On the positive side for the Brits, the lack of concern for the text has certainly contributed to what Ian Richardson described as an 'irony deficiency' among American actors: 'English acting tends to be understated and depends heavily on nuance and irony' – which is why he finds that Chekhov has always been popular in England. 'I would say that, to the British, Americans in general seem to suffer from a serious irony deficiency.'[240]

Perhaps, for the sake of international understanding, the last word on the topic should be left to Dame Judi Dench, who is popular on both sides of the Atlantic, and in film and television and on the stage. She admits that she does not know what the difference is between good American acting and good British acting: 'It all has to come down to the same thing: does it make you believe in that person?'[241]

DOING SHAKESPEARE

Feelings about Shakespeare's plays very often depend on how one is introduced to them. Many who have to struggle through at least one of them as a set text at school are put off for life, but if one is lucky enough to have been introduced to the Bard by a sensitive, enthusiastic and imaginative teacher it can be the start of a life-long love affair. Eileen Atkins tells of how a teacher helped her improve her speaking voice, partly by introducing her to some speeches from Shakespeare. He introduced her to Shakespeare in such a painless way that she never worried about it again.[242] Many young actors nowadays, however, who have not had the advantage of such familiarity with his works from an early age, often find the complexity, obscurity and poetic structure difficult to master. Speaking in the late 1990s, Jane Lapotaire said that she had noticed a deterioration in the way the language was spoken in the Royal Shakespeare Company. She felt that this was because most drama schools train people mainly for television, so that they do not know how to project or speak blank verse. When they arrive at the RSC, many have never even been in a play by Shakespeare. Citing further the breakdown of the repertory system in Britain, she concludes that this has resulted in all our cultural inheritance being undermined.[243] And if young British actors are having problems, it is no wonder that many American actors do. Of Mel Gibson's performance as Hamlet, Lapotaire commented that it was a one-dimensional performance because he had not had the experience of speaking Shakespeare's language over many years. He did not know that you had to run a line through, and then take the break. Basically, she feels that you cannot apply the Method approach – what she describes as just behaving in front of the camera, or 'behaviourism' – to playing Shakespeare, because you have to think as you speak in Shakespeare plays. 'If you do *behaviourism*, with Shakespeare, you'd be in the theatre for four months.'[244]

Following the clues

Many experienced actors have found that there are not so many differences between the demands of performing Shakespeare's prose and those of performing his verse. Liev Schreiber has said that he does not play prose and verse very differently from each other. You just have to follow the clues in the text.[245] Although Shakespeare as a writer is demanding, he is also generous to the actor. Patricia Hayes said that Shakespeare gives wonderful opportunities to actors, because he tells you what the person is thinking and feeling. But there is still freedom for individual characterisation.[246]

Harry Andrews found that it was important to maintain the flow in Shakespeare's long speeches. While you must take a breath, you should not stop suddenly. Breaking up lines ruins the sense. He discovered that respecting the punctuation helped. It is important to maintain the sense of a line, and respect the poetry, even when it's blank verse.[247]

Maintaining the flow

While recognising the need to maintain the flow, Robert Stephens does consider it necessary to break up long speeches, at least mentally, if not in delivery. He believes that you should never treat a long speech as a long speech, because, as in real life, people change their minds and are reminded of something else. It helps to fragment it into thoughts, which makes it sound natural.[248] It can be fatal to speak the lines self-consciously as verse. Madoline Thomas has said that, if it is said naturally, it will be all right. But some people develop a sing-song tone because they know that it is verse.[249] Another way of putting this is to stress that the meaning must be paramount, and not the rhythm of the verse. In the words of Margaret Tyzack: 'Intent must overwhelm the verse... It must never become music and, if intent does overwhelm it, it never will.'[250]

Those daunted by Shakespeare often tend to respect every word too much. The emphasis has to be selective. Gwen Ffrangcon-Davies recalls the famous director Tyrone Guthrie saying: 'Don't hit every word, take it in a sweep, making up your mind which will be the high spot. Make for that and then let the rest go.'[251]

Iambic pentameters

Despite the overall concern for flow and meaning, the basic verse structure cannot – and, as many actors would agree, should not – be ignored. It does not necessarily involve learning a set of rules, but it must involve some sensitivity to the rhythms. Fabia Drake admits to not being interested in rules of verse as such, but it is important to her how she handles the beat of the line: 'You listen for the rhythm, which is inescapable... You can't make a mistake once you are aware of the rhythm.' All other technical features of the verse are secondary for her. She is not interested in any other things, such as broken lines, end-stopping, rhyming couplets and feminine endings.[252] For Ian Richardson, it was possible to combine respect for the verse structure with a form of naturalism. Referring to a speech in *Two Gentlemen of Verona*, he has said that, if you say a line with upward inflections until the last part, you are not simply declaiming but speaking Shakespeare. 'When you throw out an acknowledgement of the iambic pentameter, you throw out the heart of the text.'[253]

Peter Barkworth has given a good tip for handling Shakespeare's verse. One part of the actor's mind, of his or her conception of the character being played, should be to think of oneself as a poet, to think poetically. This is necessary if one is to capture also what Barkworth calls the 'voice of the author'. You must imagine yourself to be a poet and not merely quoting one.[254]

'You can't go very far wrong.'

A final word of encouragement to actors still nervous of taking on Shakespeare comes from Michael Hordern, who, as other actors have done, learned to trust an intuitive feel for the verse rhythms: if you are reasonably intelligent and can read and speak English, then verse-speaking should be completely instinctive. 'As long as you are speaking the verse of somebody who knows how to write it, like William Shakespeare, you can't go very far wrong.'[255]

GOING PROFESSIONAL

Most of what has been written hitherto in this book has been designed to be of interest to both keen amateur and would-be professional actor alike. A friend who was experienced in teaching drama in an academic setting once expressed the opinion that amateurism and professionalism were essentially attitudes of mind, and that a good amateur actor could, and often did, have a professional attitude to developing his or her role. The only real difference was that the professional got paid for their trouble. However, as many professional actors have revealed in this book, there are certain techniques and physical abilities which one can really only learn through professional training. To perform nightly (not to mention in matinees) over long periods the actor needs to be able to use voice and body efficiently without exhausting them too soon, and to be able to maintain constantly a high quality of performance. The actor needs, in short, stamina.

The keen amateur actor who considers going professional needs to bear in mind that it will be a gruelling and insecure life, with no certainty of regular income.

TO BE OR NOT TO BE

Whether to take the risk of seeking professional employment as an actor, and perhaps devote the rest of one's life to it, is a question which needs profound and careful consideration. The decision should not be taken lightly. The present writer once knew a successful, middle-aged businessman who opted to give up his secure, well-paid job and, after a short acting course, endeavoured to become a professional actor. He only managed to obtain work very occasionally, but did not have to worry about this too much as he was single, had a small fortune behind him, and could thus cushion himself against long periods of unemployment. Few people are in such fortunate circumstances. It is not surprising, therefore, that not many people over the age of 30 are willing to take the risk and become actors. It is far better, and safer, to start young and learn survival techniques early.

Most books providing practical guidance for would-be actors are therefore aimed at the young: school leavers or students. Many of the actors of the older generation have gone through the experience of repertory theatre and mastered the art through doing it the hard way, rehearsing and learning the lines for one play in the daytime while performing in another play in the evenings, non-stop for months on end. There are few such old stagers around nowadays, and even fewer repertory companies still functioning. To obtain the necessary experience, training and gain access to the acting job market today it is essential to have made one's way through a good drama school. Some guidance on these is provided in the next section. Before getting to the stage of selecting a school, however, it is wise to consider whether one is really ready for the insecurity of the actor's lifestyle. Reading a few good books by experienced actors will help in the decision-making process.

A useful place to start is *So You Want To Be An Actor* by the successful husband and wife acting team Timothy West and Prunella Scales. They must have got it all reasonably right, because their son Samuel West has also become a successful actor. They provide lots of sound, hard-hitting, frank advice to the would-be actor: 'Your development will largely depend on luck, fashion, who you know, what you look like, and the general state of the business. It's tough, but there it is.' A little later they add, referring to the situation just before the book was published in 2005: 'Unemployment statistics in the profession are hard to ascertain accurately, but a recent Equity survey showed that only some 20 per cent of members worked more than 30 weeks a year, while 48 per cent worked fewer than 11 weeks.'[256] Equally firmly, they advise against studying drama as an academic subject:

Don't go to a Child Acting School, but get as broad an education as you can, and don't do 'Drama' as an academic subject. A professional actor doesn't need to know about Drama, but about Life. You need to observe and understand 'real' people. If you go on to university, read English, History, Music, a foreign language, or even a scientific subject. Do as much acting as you can in your free time or out of school and university hours.[257]

West and Scales also provide much constructive advice for the difficult period after graduation from drama training: how to get an agent, advertising yourself, handling interviews and auditions, obtaining some financial security, maintaining good physical health, and joining the actors' union Equity. They also give excellent advice on how to cope with those difficult periods of unemployment.

Another excellent book, recommended by many actors and teachers alike, is the actor Clive Swift's *The Job of Acting*. He provides especially useful advice on good ways to make oneself known to prospective employers and write effective letters to agents, producers and the like, and also how to get a good portfolio of photographs, etc. Peter Barkworth's book, *About Acting*, in addition to providing many extremely helpful tips on technique, also contains some wise reflections on the problems of survival in the profession.

Such books (and others as indicated in the Resources section) should be required reading for all those who are considering taking the plunge into the uncertain, though infinitely rewarding, life of the professional actor.

TRAINING

It is difficult to give detailed advice about training courses and drama schools, precisely because, if they are any good, they will be constantly changing and updating their courses, utilising the latest techniques and facilities, modifying methods in accordance with experience, etc. As with all educational institutions, the quality of the training will vary and change as the teachers come and go. Large, well-established institutions can sometimes seem impersonal, while the small, intimate school may have much to recommend it, but may not be able to afford extensive resources.

The most useful publication for those wishing to select a drama school suitable to their needs is *Contacts*, published annually by The Spotlight. *Contacts* contains, amongst other valuable information, a list of all the drama schools which together make up the 'Conference of Drama Schools' (the CDS). Details of these are supplied in the Resources section of the present book.

To obtain funding for one's studies is easier nowadays than it used to be, but can be complicated and varied. Also the conditions and general regulations governing funding, as well as the conditions of acceptance imposed by the various schools, will naturally vary from year to year. There is therefore little point in including current conditions and regulations in this book, as they would soon lose their validity. There are various student-loan schemes and scholarships on offer. West and Scales provide some guidance on those available at the time their book was published (2005). It is also worth noting that, apart from the 22 odd drama schools listed as belonging to the CDS in a recent count, there are hundreds of other organisations and independent teachers devoted to drama training, which are listed in *Contacts*. It can be difficult to judge between them and decide which to approach. West and Scales provide some helpful tips on how to make a start:

Study the list of schools, write to a few you like the look of and ask for a prospectus from each, or visit their website. Read this material carefully, and having done so, make a shortlist of three or four, and write to them asking for an interview and audition. If your application is granted, they'll tell you the sort of thing they will expect you to prepare for the audition, and will warn you that they charge a fee.[258]

Finally, it should be stressed that there are good and bad things about all training courses. When actors talk of their experiences at RADA, LAMDA, Central School, and all the other well-known and not so well-known drama schools, it is clear that, while they may have criticisms to make, they also acquired many useful skills and insights in the process. Above all, the process of training helps them to understand their own motivations in acting, what they can and cannot do with their bodies, and how to combine intuition with intellectual insight in developing a role and successfully projecting the result to an audience. One can see that what has happened in the process of training for most actors is a deconstruction and reconstruction of the self, acquainting an actor with the component parts of his or her own personality, which can then be used to put together and embody given roles in plays. The actor Conrad Nelson has said that, in talking to many actors over the years about their experiences at drama school, he found that one aspect of these experiences was common – 'the sense that they were brutally taken apart and then rebuilt, as though certain things had to be knocked out of them before they would make acceptable actors'.[259]

Jane Lapotaire has put it all into perspective: 'Drama school doesn't get rid of short-comings, it just presents your problems to you, deconstructs you, if you like, and the rest of your life is spent trying to hide the faults and reconstruct... The truth is you leave drama school knowing where those flaws are.'[260]

RESOURCES

HISTORY OF ACTING

Cole, Toby and Krich Chinoy, Helen (Eds), *Actors on Acting*, New York: Crown Publishers, 1962 (first edition 1949)

INTERVIEWS WITH ACTORS

Haill, Lyn (Ed), *Actors Speaking*, London: Oberon Books, 2007

Luckhurst, Mary and Veltman, Chloe (Eds), *On Acting*, London: Faber and Faber, 2001

Zucker, Carole, *In the Company of Actors*, London: A&C Black Ltd, 1999

ACTORS ON ACTING

Callow, Simon, *Being an Actor*, London: Penguin, 1995 (first published 1984)

Cole, Toby and Krich Chinoy, Helen (Eds), *Actors on Acting*, New York: Crown Publishers, 1962 (first edition 1949)

Gielgud, John, with Miller, John, *Acting Shakespeare*, London: Pan Books, 1997

Olivier, Laurence, *On Acting*, London: Sceptre, imprint of Hodder and Stoughton Ltd, 1987

Redgrave, Michael, *The Actor's Ways and Means*, London: Nick Hern Books, 1995

ADVICE ON ACTING

Barkworth, Peter, *About Acting*, London: Methuen Drama, 2001

Chekhov, Michael, *On the Technique of Acting*, London: Collins, 1993 (first published 1942)

Hagen, Uta, with Frankel, Haskel, *Respect for Acting*, USA: Wiley, 2008 (first published 1973)

Mamet, David, *True and False, Heresy and Common Sense for the Actor*, London: Faber and Faber, 1997

THEORY OF ACTING

Stanislavsky, Constantin, *An Actor Prepares*, London: Methuen Drama, 1988

Stanislavsky, Constantin, *An Actor's Handbook*, London: Methuen Drama, 1990

Stanislavsky, Constantin, *Building a Character*, London: Methuen Drama, 1988

Stanislavsky, Constantin, *Creating a Role*, London: Mentor, 1968

OTHER BOOKS ON ACTING AND RELATED TOPICS

Brook, Peter, *There Are No Secrets: Thoughts on Acting and Theatre*, London: Methuen Drama, 1995

Gibson, Joy Leslie, *Ian McKellen*, London: Weidenfeld and Nicholson, 1986

Guinness, Alec, *Blessings in Disguise*, London: Penguin, 1997

GOING PROFESSIONAL

Scales, Prunella and West, Timothy, *So You Want To Be An Actor?* London: Nick Hern Books, 2005

Swift, Clive, *The Job of Acting*, London: Harrap, 1976

TRAINING

Barker, Clive, *Theatre Games, A New Approach to Drama Training*, London: Methuen Drama, 1989

GENERAL RESOURCE AND REFERENCE BOOKS

Contacts, a yearbook published by 'The Spotlight', London. It is described by its publishers as 'the essential handbook for everyone working or wanting to work in the entertainment industry', and has been a regular annual publication since 1947, containing over 5,000 listings, which are updated annually. It is truly the most comprehensive work of reference available on all aspects of the performing arts, and includes advice on choosing suitable drama training. www.spotlight.com

Dunmore, Simon and Piper, Andrew, *Actors' Yearbook*, London: Methuen Drama, A&C Black (annually). According to the editors, this yearbook 'contains thousands of contacts, from agents to production companies, with detailed entries and guidance on how to make your approach'. The 2008 edition contained, for example, a foreword by Simon Callow stressing how important it is for actors to learn how to sell themselves. The introduction emphasises that training is essential for getting a job nowadays, as producers and directors want to be sure that they can rely on acquired techniques. It also stresses that it is important to choose a professionally recognised training course, and lists those that are. There are also useful essays on such topics as choosing effective audition speeches, finding funding for productions, fringe theatre, working in TV and radio, advice for disabled actors, etc.

The Conference of Drama Schools, CDS Guide to Professional Training in Drama and Technical Theatre. This brochure, published annually, lists all the drama schools and drama training institutes which are members of the conference. In 2007 this was 22 institutions, which offered vocational training for actors. All the members emphasise the importance of practical training as well as academic qualifications. Copies of the brochure can be obtained from French's Theatre Bookshop: www.samuelfrench-london.co.uk (email: theatre@samuelfrench-london.co.uk). The latest information on CDS schools, a downloadable version of the guide and a searchable database can be found on their website: www.drama.ac.uk

PERIODICALS

The Stage, published weekly. It is described as 'a weekly for the entertainment industry' and, while aimed at the professional, contains articles on acting, theatre services and media of interest to the amateur. There is also information on drama schools, relevant university courses, etc. www.thestage.co.uk

NOTES

1   Cole, Toby and Krich Chinoy, Helen (Eds), *Actors on Acting*, New York: Crown Publishers, 1962 (first published 1949), 3

2   Ibid, 5

3   Ibid

4   Ibid

5   Cicero, *Cicero on Oratory and Orators,* translation by Watson, JS, London: George Bell and Sons, 1876 (in AOA, 23)

6   Ibid

7   Lucian, *The Works of Lucian of Samosata*, translation by Fowler, HW and FG, Oxford: Clarendon, 1905, 238–63, passim

8   Ibid

9   Ibid

10   Ibid

11   Cole & Krich Chinoy, op cit, 36

12   Mantzius, Karl, *A History of Theatrical Art in Ancient and Modern Times*, translation by von Cossel, Louise, New York: Peter Smith, 1937, vol II, 9–10

13   Cole & Krich Chinoy, op cit, 91

14   Flecknoe, Richard, 'The Acting of Richard Burbage' in Chambers, EK, *The Elizabethan Stage*, Oxford: Clarendon, 1923, vol IV, 370

15 Webster, John, 'An Excellent Actor', (written 1815), in
    Rimbault, EF (Ed), *The Miscellaneous Works in Prose and Verse
    of Sir Thomas Overbury*, London: John Russell Smith, 1856,
    147–8

16 Shergold, ND, *A History of the Spanish Stage: From Medieval
    Times Until the End of the Seventeenth Century*, Oxford: OUP,
    1967, 520

17 Bates, Alfred (Ed), *The Drama: Its History, Literature and
    Influence on Civilisation*, London: Historical Publishing
    Company, 1906, vol 6, 21–3

18 Gildon, Charles, *The Life of Mr Thomas Betterton, the Late
    Eminent Tragedian. Wherein the Action and Utterance of the
    Stage, Bar, and Pulpit are distinctly Considered* (including the
    manual ascribed to Betterton), London: Robert Gosling, 1710,
    11–43, passim

19 Cibber, Colley, *Colley Cibber's Apology for his Life*, London: JM
    Dent and Sons Ltd, (date unavailable), 56–93, 294–7, passim

20 Ibid

21 Ibid

22 Ibid

23 Cole & Krich Chinoy, op cit, 121

24 Macklin, Charles, 'The Art and Duty of an Actor' in Kirkman,
    JT, *Memoirs of the Life of Charles Macklin, Esq, principally
    compiled from his own papers and memorandums*, London:
    Lockington, Allen and Company, 1799, vol I, 362–6

25 Olivier, Laurence, *On Acting*, London: Sceptre, imprint of
    Hodder and Stoughton Ltd, 1987, 40

26 Cole & Krich Chinoy, op cit, 141

27 Ibid, 148

28 Diderot, Denis, *The Paradox of Acting*, translation by Pollock,
    WH, London: Chatto and Windus, 1883, 6–25, passim

29 Ibid

30 Cole & Krich Chinoy, op cit, 178

31 Ibid, 235

32 Lessing, GE, *Selected Prose Works of GE Lessing*, translation
    by Beasley, EC and Zimmern, H, edited by Bell, Edward,
    London: George Bell and Sons, 1879, 240–8

33 Cole & Krich Chinoy, op cit, 415

34 Ibid, 297

35 Ibid

36 Ibid, 298

37 Ibid

38 Ibid

39 Ibid, 293

40 Ibid, 294

41 Ibid, 347

42 Shaw, George Bernard, 'From the Point of View of a Playwright'
    in Beerbohm, Max, *Herbert Beerbohm Tree: Some Memories of
    Him and His Art*, London: Hutchinson (date unavailable),
    240–3

43 Ibid

44 Cole & Krich Chinoy, op cit, 150

45 Ibid, 195

46 Ibid, 207 (two quotes)

47 Bernhardt, Sarah, *The Art of the Theatre*, London: G Bles,
    1924, 103–6

48 Cole & Krich Chinoy, op cit, 191

49 Devrient, Eduard, *Bemerkungen zur Novelle*, in Rein,
    Ferdinand, *Eduard Devrient als Oberregisseur in Dresden von
    1844–1846*, Altenburg, Germany: Stephan Geibel and Co,
    1931, 41

50 Cole & Krich Chinoy, op cit, 237

51 Ibid, 264

52 Ibid, 415

53 Ibid, 422

54 Ibid, 354

[55] Fay, WG, *Merely Players*, London: Rich and Cowan, 1932, 19–23

[56] Cole & Krich Chinoy, op cit, 230

[57] Ibid, 239

[58] Ibid, 417

[59] Ibid, 425 (both quotes)

[60] Stanislavsky, Constantin, 'The Beginnings of My System' in *My Life in Art*, translation by Robbins, JJ, New York: Theatre Art Books, 1948, 458–67

[61] Ibid

[62] Cole & Krich Chinoy, op cit, 420

[63] Ibid

[64] Eisenstein, Sergei, *The Film Sense*, translation by Leyda, J, New York: Harcourt, Brace and Co, 1942, 17–18

[65] Luckhurst, Mary and Veltman, Chloe (Eds), *On Acting*, London: Faber and Faber, 2001, 8

[66] Callow, Simon, *Being an Actor*, London: Penguin, 1995 (first published 1984), 178

[67] Barkworth, Peter, *About Acting*, London: Methuen Drama, 2001, 183

[68] Luckhurst & Veltman, op cit, 16

[69] Ibid, 122

[70] Ibid

[71] Barkworth, op cit, 215

[72] Zucker, Carole, *In the Company of Actors*, London: A&C Black Ltd, 1999, 12

[73] Callow, op cit, 31

[74] Zucker, op cit, 7 (both quotes)

[75] Ibid, 65

[76] Ibid, 48

[77] Ibid, 45

[78] Ibid, 157

[79] Luckhurst & Veltman, op cit, 132

80 Zucker, op cit, 125

81 Luckhurst & Veltman, op cit, 142

82 Zucker, op cit, 155

83 Callow, op cit, 201

84 Zucker, op cit, 89

85 Ibid, 135

86 Ibid, 172

87 Luckhurst & Veltman, op cit, 77

88 Ibid, 86

89 Ibid, 95

90 Ibid, 111

91 Haill, Lyn, *Actors Speaking*, London: Oberon Books, 2007, 57

92 Ibid, 119

93 Barkworth, op cit, 13–14

94 Ibid, 179

95 Ibid, 215

96 Zucker, op cit, 6

97 Luckhurst & Veltman, op cit, 143

98 Zucker, op cit, 13

99 Ibid, 21

100 Ibid, 50

101 Ibid, 51

102 Ibid, 103

103 Ibid, 81–2

104 Ibid, 97

105 Ibid, 114

106 Ibid, 132

107 Ibid, 24

108 Ibid, 56–7

109 Ibid, 69

110 Ibid, 176

111 Luckhurst & Veltman, op cit, 113

112 Zucker, op cit, 136

[113] Luckhurst & Veltman, op cit, 28

[114] Barkworth, op cit, 181–2

[115] Zucker, op cit, 188

[116] Ibid, 190

[117] Barkworth, op cit, 15

[118] Zucker, op cit, 206

[119] Ibid, 216

[120] Haill, op cit, 40

[121] Zucker, op cit, 33

[122] Ibid

[123] Ibid, 183–4

[124] Luckhurst & Veltman, op cit, 140

[125] Ibid, 89

[126] Ibid, 62

[127] Zucker, op cit, 34

[128] Ibid, 49

[129] Ibid, 189

[130] Ibid, 127

[131] Ibid, 128

[132] Ibid, 199

[133] Haill, op cit, 36

[134] Ibid, 41

[135] Ibid, 127

[136] Ibid, 60

[137] Ibid, 76

[138] Ibid, 94

[139] Ibid, 61

[140] Ibid, 101

[141] Ibid, 49

[142] Ibid, 95 (both quotes)

[143] Ibid, 137–8

[144] Barker, Clive, *Theatre Games*, London: Methuen Drama, 1989, 196

145 Redgrave, Michael, *The Actor's Ways and Means*, London: Nick Hern Books,1995, 115

146 Ibid, 113

147 Guinness, Alec, *Blessings in Disguise*, London: Penguin, 1997, 54–5

148 Barker, op cit, 184–6

149 Haill, op cit, 74

150 Gielgud, John, *Acting Shakespeare*, London: Pan Books, 1997, 31–2

151 Haill, op cit, 30

152 Barker, op cit, 182– 3 (two quotes)

153 Stanislavsky, Constantin, 'Building a Character' in *An Actor's Handbook*, London: Methuen Drama, 1990, 86–7

154 Zucker, op cit, 22

155 Ibid, 14

156 Haill, op cit, 126

157 Luckhurst & Veltman, op cit, 67

158 Zucker, op cit, 16

159 Ibid, 69

160 Barkworth, op cit, 18 & 19

161 Haill, op cit, 50 & 51

162 Callow, op cit, 89

163 Zucker, op cit, 8

164 Ibid, 208

165 Ibid, 101

166 Luckhurst & Veltman, op cit, 81

167 Barkworth, op cit, 26

168 Zucker, op cit, 10

169 Luckhurst & Veltman, op cit, 39

170 Barkworth, op cit, 24

171 Zucker, op cit, 16

172 Haill, op cit, 43

173 Zucker, op cit, 137

174 Ibid, 222

175 Luckhurst & Veltman, op cit, 129

176 Ibid, 13–14

177 Zucker, op cit, 36

178 Luckhurst & Veltman, op cit, 85

179 Zucker, op cit, 22

180 Ibid, 59

181 Ibid, 167

182 Ibid, 195

183 Luckhurst & Veltman, op cit, 19

184 Zucker, op cit, 168

185 Haill, op cit, 70

186 Barkworth, op cit, 196

187 Ibid, 170

188 Zucker, op cit, 9

189 Ibid, 61

190 Ibid, 152

191 Ibid, 30

192 Ibid, 46

193 Luckhurst & Veltman, op cit, 75

194 Ibid, 80–1

195 Ibid, 119

196 Barkworth, op cit, 75

197 Luckhurst & Veltman, op cit, 136

198 Haill, op cit, 88

199 Ibid, 100

200 Ibid, 121

201 Barkworth, op cit, 191–2

202 Ibid, 190

203 Ibid, 183–4

204 Haill, op cit, 80

205 Barkworth, op cit, 220

206 Ibid, 63

207 Ibid, 63–6

208 Ibid, 264

209 Haill, op cit, 126

210 Barkworth, op cit, 257

211 Ibid, 63

212 Zucker, op cit, 50

213 Ibid, 132

214 Ibid, 61

215 Luckhurst & Veltman, op cit, 142

216 Zucker, op cit, 202

217 Ibid, 191

218 Ibid, 223

219 Luckhurst & Veltman, op cit, 77

220 Zucker, op cit, 179

221 Luckhurst & Veltman, op cit, 69

222 Ibid, 86

223 Ibid, 114

224 Ibid, 150

225 Ibid, 99

226 Zucker, op cit, 70

227 Barkworth, op cit, 72

228 Ibid, 227–8

229 Ibid, 248

230 Zucker, op cit, 8–9

231 Ibid, 88

232 Ibid, 107

233 Ibid, 196

234 Ibid, 211

235 Haill, op cit, 144

236 Zucker, op cit, 94–5

237 Ibid, 225

238 Luckhurst & Veltman, op cit, 116

239 Zucker, op cit, 90

[240] Ibid, 139

[241] Ibid, 52

[242] Ibid, 3

[243] Ibid, 80

[244] Ibid, 88 & 89

[245] Luckhurst & Veltman, op cit, 113

[246] Haill, op cit, 99

[247] Ibid, 33

[248] Ibid, 128

[249] Ibid, 137

[250] Ibid, 142

[251] Ibid, 57

[252] Ibid, 49–50 (two quotes)

[253] Zucker, op cit, 129

[254] Barkworth, op cit, 13

[255] Haill, op cit, 111

[256] Scales, Prunella and West, Samuel, *So You Want To Be An Actor?*, London: Nick Hern Books, 2005, 4 (two quotes)

[257] Ibid, 5–6

[258] Ibid, 13

[259] Luckhurst & Veltman, op cit, 87

[260] Zucker, op cit, 79–80

INDEX

kamera BOOKS &
creative ESSENTIALS

'an exc... ...ll
be wel... ...e.'

don

nd

ntion

of

Directs documents a heroic moment in the life of a great artist.

978-1-84243-227-3 £25
978-1-84243-228-0 £12.99

www.kamerabooks.com